FOX-TERRIER BREEDING
(SMOOTH AND WIRE)

East Sussex Hounds at Herstmonceux

FOX-TERRIER BREEDING

(SMOOTH AND WIRE)
THE LINE AND FAMILY METHOD

BY

The Rev. ROSSLYN BRUCE
D.D. (OXON), F.L.S.

Chaplain to the Royal Horse Artillery (T.); Rector of Herstmonceux, Sussex

Acknowledgment.

OUR delightful Frontispiece lately appeared by chance in the *Sussex County Herald*, and the appropriate position of a large and small Fox-terrier suggested its introduction to this book, to which the Editor courteously agreed. Messrs. HEDGES, of Lytham, have kindly allowed the use of most of the photographs, and Mr. REVELEY, of Wantage, was equally obliging: thanks are due to them, and also to those who have corrected the proofs; and Mr. DUKES and Mr. STANLEY, among many others, have also given very useful help.

ROSSLYN BRUCE.

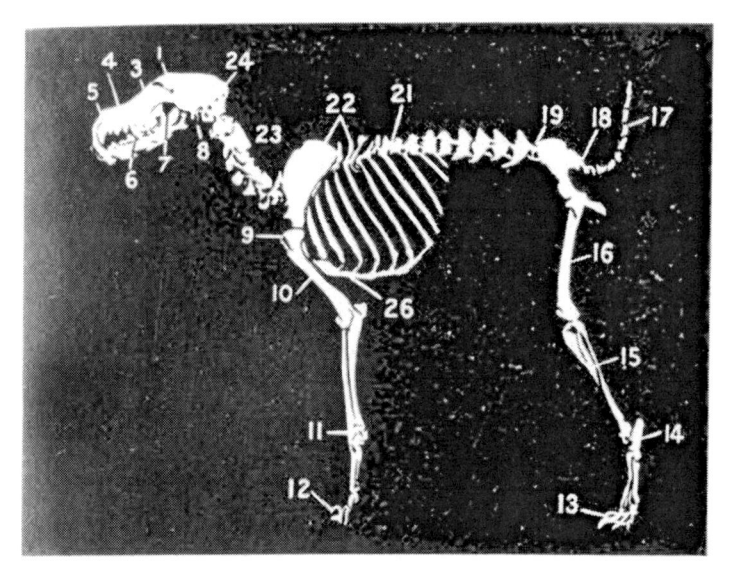

FOX-TERRIER BONE.

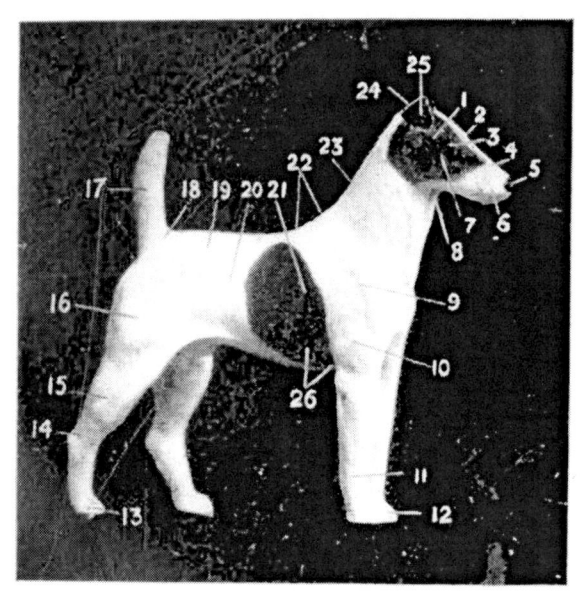

1. Skull	H	10. Elbow	S	19. Loin	R
2. Stop	H	11. Knee	L	20. Back Rib	R
3. Eye	H	12. Pad	L	21. Ribs	R
4. Forehead	H	13. Hind pad	L	22. Withers	S
5. Nose	H	14. Hock	O	23. Crest	N
6. Lip	H	15. Second Thigh	O	24. Occiput	H
7. Cheek	H	16. Thigh	O	25. Ear	H
8. Throat	N	17. Tail	T	26. Brisket	S
9. Shoulder	S	18. Root of Tail	R		

CONTENTS.

Chapter		Page
I	Introduction	17
II	Points of the Fox-terrier	25
III	Systematic Breeding	37
IV	Lines and Families	53
V	Lines of Sires	62
VI	Families of Dams	74
VII	Champions of the 20th Century to 1931	112
VIII	Challenge Certificates	120
IX	Fox-terrier Points	125
X	Notes by the Way	128
	Index to Champions	151

PICTURE SHOWING AN EARLY FOX-TERRIER, circa 1750.
By George Stubbs, 1724-1806.

LIST OF ILLUSTRATIONS.

	PAGE
EAST SUSSEX HUNT ...	*Frontispiece*
FOX-TERRIER BONE! ...	7
FOX-TERRIER POINTS ...	7
AN EARLY FOX-TERRIER ...	11
VIPER ...	15
CH DONNA'S DOUBLE ...	19
CH CHOICEST DONNA OF NOTTS ...	19
CH. DUSKY DINAH ...	23
AVON MIONE ...	23
FOILER, So ...	27
HOGNASTON DICK, So ...	27
DICKON, So ...	31
CH. SPLINTER, So ...	31
VESUVIAN, So ...	35
CH. VENIO, So ...	35
VISTO, So ...	39
DARK BLUE, So ...	39
CH OXONIAN, So ...	43
CH. ORKNEY, So ...	43
CH. ORKADIAN, So ...	47
CH CROMWELL OCHRE, So ...	51
CROMWELL OCHRE'S LEGACY, So ...	55
CROMWELL RAW UMBER, So ...	55
KIDDER KARZAN, So ...	59
CH. LITTLE ARISTOCRAT, So ...	63
CH. SELECTA IDEAL, So ...	67
CH. AVON STERLING, So ...	71
CH. SELECTA ALL ALONE, So ...	71
BELGRAVE JOE, Jr ...	75
CH RESULT, Jr ...	75
D'ORSAY'S DOUBLE, Jr ...	79
CH. CAPT. DOUBLE, Jr ...	79
CH. RABY GALLIARD, Jr ...	83
CH. DANDYFORD, Jr ...	83
CH. KINVER, Jr. ...	87
CH. ARROGANT ALBINO, Jr ...	91
CH. DOMINIE, Jd ...	97
DUSKY DIVER, Jd ...	97
CH. DARRELL, Jd ...	101
DUSKY D'ORSAY, T ...	101
"GOOD WORK!" ...	129
A NURSERY PARTY ...	129
MR. REDMOND ...	139

Viper, 1796. *Painted by Sartorius*

CHAPTER I.

Introduction.

"If you wish to write, read all that has been written," said a wise old Roman two thousand years ago. His advice applies to our subject, and ro one will wisely rush into print upon fox-terriers till he has scanned the work of his forerunners. It will astonish a novice to know that the writer has one hundred and twenty-seven volumes on his shelves, all of which deal, more or less, with smooth fox-terriers, past and present, and that he frequently refers to nearly all of them; these are all in English, but there is also a considerable amount of continental literature, which vies in excellence and finish with our best British efforts.

But it is the British on which a few lines of guidance will be of value to our readers. To begin with, there are some excellent articles, written some time ago, such as Mr. Desmond O'Connell's eight large pages, with nine illustrations, in Cassell's "New Book of the Dog" (vol. III), 1912; Mr. J. C. Tinne's excellent twenty pages, with twenty-three illustrations, in the "Kennel Encyclopædia" (vol. II), 1908; Mr. Vero Shaw's twenty-six pages, with three pictures, in "The Illustrated Book of the Dog" (1881); all of these are of permanent interest, for though the latter was written in 1881, it includes a scale of merits written by Mr. Redmond, to which all would probably subscribe to-day, and most of the early history has never been rewritten.

Perhaps the most ambitiously produced book of all is "The Fox-terrier," by Mr. Rawdon Lee, published in 1889, with fifteen excellent pictures by Mr. Arthur Wardle; much of this book is revised and reproduced in "Modern Dogs" (Terriers), third edition (1903), which contains fifty pages on "The Fox-terrier," followed by thirty on "The Wire-haired Fox-terrier." Then followed Mr. Sidney Castle's "Monograph on the Fox-terrier," a limp cloth bound book of seventy pages, with five illustrations; this volume was revised and partly rewritten by Mr. Theo. Marples, and produced as a joint compilation of about ninety pages with ten illustrations, in 1916, and it is to-day most excellent and instructive reading. There is also a little book called " The Fox-terrier " in Upcott Gill's " Monographs of British Dogs " series, written by the late Mr. Hugh Dalziel ; it contains much interesting matter, including twenty-seven pages on smooths and seven on wires, and some forty more on general fox-terrier advice, and a few good pictures and pedigrees. It is marred, perhaps, by several pages of unbridled and contemptuous abuse of another fox-terrier expert, who, whatever his faults, spent his whole life among fox-terriers, and was not so ignorant as Mr. Dalziel would have us believe. Then there are the late Mr. Martin's excellent serial articles published in a monthly magazine, " The Kennel."

Then, again, there is a little brochure called " The Perfect Fox-terrier," by the late Mr. Astley, a Lancashire all-round dog judge, with a gift for journalism ; it is a curious mixture, containing, frankly, some very thin stuff, but not without some telling sentences to illustrate its cleverly-drawn outlines of terrier points. The Rev. A. J. Skinner's " Popular Fox-terrier " is a much pleasanter and more modern book.

Lastly, there are the twenty-two annual volumes of " The Fox-terrier Chronicle," which contain a mass of old-time lore and much material of a lasting value ; they cover the period for 1883 to 1905, and were issued in monthly numbers. Annuals dealing with the wires or the smooths, or both, appear most years, and often contain much that is of permanent interest, both to novices and to experts. The illustrations are of great help for purposes of comparison, especially the earlier photographs, which were far more " honest " than the more recent ones, for these tend to show a terrier not as he is, but as we dream of him.

The extent of the literature shows the enormous field over which the interest in smooth fox-terriers spreads.

Books on Heredity.

Probably the best books on breeding problems are Davenport's " Principles of Breeding," Punnett's " Mendelism," J. R. Robertson's (" Mankato ") " Heredity Applied to Race-horses," Oettingen's " Horse Breeding," Cossar Ewart's

Ch. Donna's Double, Jd 5, born 1909.

Ch. Choicest Donna of Notts, So 3, born 1927.

"Principles of Breeding," Bateson, and also Thompson, on "Heredity," and in a less ambitious line, Doncaster, and Watson and Crew, each on "Heredity," Ward Cutler on "Evolution Heredity and Variation," C. J. Davies on "The Theory and Practise of Breeding to Type," and Christian Wriedt on "Heredity in Live Stock." Anyone who has mastered the meaning of these books, has made himself a promising student, and should be as qualified as he ever will be to select the right stud dog for his needs each spring ; he will not breed in autumn !

TYPE AND ORIGIN.

It is very striking how the character and appearance of individual terriers become matter of common knowledge and general interest. For years a " D'Orsay marked " head was a familiar description, and although that excellent dog's blood (in tail male) is, I believe, totally extinct, the all-black head is now so common as to need no special designation. In this connection someone in 1923 advertised a dog " marked like Sir Julian " ; now Sir Julian's markings are not unusual, and he had not been shown since 1920, and as the advertiser lives in Durham, not only has he a good memory, but also expects it in others. Markings, however, are of very small importance.

The Duchess of Newcastle writes : " You often see beagle type appear in the large soft eye and low-set ear ; and as I have always been led to understand that beagles were used when fox-terriers were invented to aid in their production, it is not surprising when these points appear again at times, although the origin has been lost in the dim past."

This tradition of a beagle cross is of great interest : it is to be found among those writers who date the origin of the fox-terrier at about 1860, when the existing lines and families began to be. Thus Mr. Rawdon Lee, writing in 1889, says of the " rich tan and black," " originally these gaudy colours were produced by some beagle blood, which I fancy came to be infused about thirty years ago. The large, flapping, almost hound-like ears, which still occasionally crop up, and were excessively common twenty years ago (1870), likewise suggest this beagle cross." Mr. Lee, however, continues : " An excessive size of the aural appendage is not an attribute of the

terrier proper, any more than are the hound markings."
With this we should all agree; but about this alleged beagle
extraction there is plenty of room for doubt. Many of our
readers will remember the pages of withering (if rather over-
vehement) scorn with which the late Hugh Dalziel ridiculed
those who strove to date the rise of fox-terriers at 1850 to 1860,
and he certainly had a very good case. The writer has himself
endeavoured to familiarise modern readers with the picture
of Viper, by Sartorius, painted in 1796—a very fair representation of an average fox-terrier, having, of course, no vestige of a
sign of a beagle origin. At a recent exhibition of "Conver-
sational" art, Lady Desborough showed a picture by George
Stubbs, A.R.A., painted about 1765, in which a very pleasant
little smooth fox-terrier appears as an ordinary member of a
country house scene. Let me quote the words of Mr. Darley
Matheson : " To summarise, we may say that the history of
the fox-terrier dates back for several centuries, and that
closely allied dogs existed as far back as 1400 or thereabouts."
Once at 1400, surely the Ark and the Garden of Eden are within
measurable hail, and some of us are downright "Arkites"
in the origin of fox-terrier controversy, as we believe that
while the modern fox-terrier is the highest and most finished
product of human selection, he is also very near in general
qualities to the original wild hunting quadruped, who was the
first object of man's domesticating instinct. Noah took two
good fox-terriers into the Ark !

CH. DUSKY DINAH, 8o 4, born 1921.

AVON MIONE, born 1908.
"The best Terrier I have ever seen." — *Theory.*
"The best animal, too!" — *Redmond.*

CHAPTER II.

Points of the Fox-terrier.

The Standard recommended by the Fox-terrier Club. Issued in 1876.

SMOOTH.

1. HEAD.—The *Skull* should be flat and moderately narrow, and gradually decreasing in width to the eyes. Not much "stop" should be apparent, but there should be more dip in the profile between the forehead and top jaw than is seen in the case of the greyhound.

The *Cheeks* must not be full.

The *Ears* should be V-shaped and small, of moderate thickness, and dropping forward close to the cheek, not hanging by the side of a head like a foxhound's.

The *Jaw*, upper and under, should be strong and muscular, should be of fair punishing strength, but not so in any way to resemble the greyhound or modern English terrier. There should not be much falling away below the eyes. This part of the head should, however, be moderately chiselled out, so as not to go down in a straight line like a wedge.

The *Nose*, towards which the muzzle must gradually taper, should be black.

The *Eyes* should be dark in colour, small, and rather deep set, full of fire, life, and intelligence; as nearly as possible circular in shape.

The *Teeth* should be nearly as possible level—*i.e.*, the upper teeth on the outside of the lower teeth.

2. NECK.—Should be clean and muscular, without throatiness, of fair length, and gradually widening to the shoulders.

3. SHOULDERS.—Should be long and sloping, well laid back, fine at the points, and clearly cut at the withers.

CHEST.—Deep and not broad.

4. BACK.—Should be short, straight and strong, with no appearance of slackness.

> LOIN.—Should be powerful and very slightly arched. The fore ribs should be moderately arched, the back ribs deep, and the dog should be well ribbed up.

5. HINDQUARTERS.—Should be strong and muscular, quite free from droop or crouch ; the thighs long and powerful ; hocks near the ground, the dog standing well up on them like a fox-hound, and not straight in the stifle.

6. STERN.—Should be set on rather high, and carried gaily, but not over the back or curled. It should be of good strength, anything approaching a " pipe-stopper " tail being exceptionally objectionable.

7. LEGS.—Viewed from any direction, must be straight, showing little or no appearance of an ankle in front. They should be strong in bone throughout, short and straight to pastern. Both fore and hind legs should be carried straight forward in travelling, the stifles not turned outward. The elbows should hang perpendicular to the body, working free of the side.

> FEET.—Should be round, compact, and not large. The soles hard and tough. The toes moderately arched, and turned neither in nor out.

8. COAT.—Should be straight, flat, smooth, hard, dense, and abundant. The belly and under side of the thighs should not be bare.

> COLOUR.—White should predominate ; brindle, red, or liver markings are objectionable. Otherwise this point is of little or no importance.

9. SYMMETRY, SIZE AND CHARACTER.—The dog must present a general gay, lively, and active appearance ; bone and strength in a small compass are essentials, but this must not be taken to mean that a fox-terrier should be cloggy, or in any way coarse—speed and endurance must be looked to as well as power, and the symmetry of the foxhound taken as a model. The terrier, like the hound, must on no account be leggy, nor must he be too short in the leg. He should stand like a cleverly-made hunter, covering a lot of ground, yet

FOILER. The Abraham of the So line,
by Grip, by Grove Willie, by Tartar.

HOGNASTON DICK, by Foiler's son, Hognaston
Willie.

with a short back, as before stated. He will then attain the highest degree of propelling power, together with the greatest length of stride that is compatible with the length of his body. *Weight* is not a certain criterion of a terrier's fitness for his work—general shape, size, and contour are the main points—and if a dog can gallop and stay, and follow his fox up a drain, it matters little what his weight is to a pound or so, though, roughly speaking, 15 to 16 lbs. for a bitch, and 16 to 18 lbs. for a dog in show conditions, are appropriate weights.

1. Head and Ears	15	
2. Neck	5	
3. Shoulders and Chest	10	
4. Back and Loin	10	
5. Hindquarters	15	
6. Stern	5	100
7. Legs and Feet	15	
8. Coat	10	
(Wires 15)		
9. Symmetry, Size and Character	15	
(Wires 10)		

WIREHAIRED.

This variety of the breed should resemble the smooth sort in every respect except the coat, which should be broken. The harder and more wiry the texture of the coat is the better. On no account should the dog look or feel woolly; and there should be no silky hair about the pole or elsewhere. The coat should not be too long, so as to give the dog a shaggy appearance, but at the same time it should show a marked and distinct difference all over from the smooth species.

DISQUALIFYING POINTS.

1. NOSE.—White, cherry, or spotted to a considerable extent with either of these colours.
2. EARS.—Prick, tulip or rose.
3. MOUTH.—Much undershot or much overshot.

EYES "CIRCULAR" NOT "ROUND."

Recently a very capable critic commented adversely on a bitch as being " a little round in eye," and he puzzled a student of the standard, which urges that the eye should be "as nearly as possible circular in shape." The discrepancy arises from the use of the word "round," probably avoided on purpose by the all but inspired drafter of the standard. In the dictionary round and circular would be almost identical, but in the technical language of the canine cult "round" is used, and has for generations been used, to express a certain fulness, which makes the eye appear to stand out with a bulgy effusiveness, which is just a shade pug-like, and not approved by sportsmen.

SYMMETRY.

A reference to the Fox-terrier Club's "standard" ever produces an avalanche of letters about it. A few ask where it can be had, and can receive the answer: "From this volume, or from almost any fox-terrier book"; but the majority have it and know it, and write for light upon such quaint phrases as "a pipe-stopper tail," etc., or for further enlightenment on some one or other of the seven points: (1) Head and neck; (2) shoulder; (3) ribs; (4) quarter; (5) legs and feet; (6) coat; and (7) action. The largest number ask for an enrichment of the last—(7) action—including size, on which a discussion generally arises, but the greatest point of all is symmetry.

Well, as to symmetry—which means, literally, measuring together—there is much that is common to all well-formed animals, such as a shoulder well thrown back, which is as desirable in a biped as in a quadruped, as every mother and governess testifies when she scoldingly remarks, " Gladys, you're stooping!" There is even more that is common to all four-footed animals, such as strong, muscular hindquarters; more still common to good, straight-legged terriers, who are all built on the lines of a weight-carrying hunter; and this typical symmetry is found at its best and most obvious in a smooth fox-terrier, perhaps the most compact epitome of the qualities which constitute symmetry.

Symmetry can best be judged at a little distance. A general impression cannot be absorbed so well at close quarters.

Symmetry can best be judged on level ground. A terrier

Dickon, by Hognaston Dick.

Ch. Splinter, by Dickon — The original S.

standing uphill generally looks much bigger (but often considerably better) than he really is.

Symmetry can best be judged broadside on, starting from the shoulder, as a sort of centre of gravity, and looking both fore and aft. The shoulder should lie back in as sloping a position as possible ; proficiency in judging this point—which does not permit of any very palpable divergence, and is, indeed, often almost imperceptible to the untrained eye—arises only from constantly studying it in as many terriers as possible. The shoulder bone is obscured more or less by the muscles that cover it ; but, even at the halt, an upright shoulder is a grievous eye-sore, and in walking it is a mighty handicap.

Symmetry demands that a terrier be long from chest to buttock—that is, covering plenty of ground space—but that his back or top line be very short, indicating strength. To achieve this combination the shoulder must slope, and also the thigh, viewed broadside on, must be almost as broad as possible.

Symmetry forbids that a terrier be " heavily topped "— the limbs, that is, appearing too slight for the body (like a beer barrel on four knitting needles). The fore limbs must not only be strong and round, like Norman pillars, but short and straight in all their lines, lest they show too high and too wide a display of daylight, and present that detestable " leggy " appearance which all terrier men hate.

Symmetry demands that a terrier be " well ribbed up," which indicates plenty of heart room and lungs and power to live. The hinder ribs must extend well back and be of good length. A whippet is a delightful creature to look at, and so, too, is a thorough-bred horse ; but we are dealing with terriers (who are to resemble hunters). An imaginary perpendicular line drawn in the middle of a terrier's back, half-way between withers and stern, from top to bottom, should be as long, or very nearly as long, as any similar line drawn nearer the withers. Then, if the under line continues without a kink up, the body has no " tucked up " appearance and the whole is symmetrical.

Symmetry demands a " good set-on " at three points : (1) The joint of head and neck ; (2) the adjustment of neck and shoulder ; and (3) the position and direction of the terrier's flag. Each of these is often referred to as the " set-on," though recently I have noticed among terrier-men that the third is generally intended. All are equally necessary to symmetry.

That heads should be long and lean and strong (heavens ! who wants a *weak* head ?) ; that necks should be long and slightly arched ; that ears should be V-shaped and small ; that eyes should be bright and dark and small ; that mouths should be straight and underjaws strong ; that coats should be hard and straight and smooth and abundant ; that feet should be deep and small and circular—these are all points which bear upon the impression of symmetry which the broadside view presents. But a complete conception can only be formed of a terrier's symmetry when a glance both at his front, at rest and in action, and at his back view in the same two positions has assured us that he stands straight, and that he moves with rhythm ; and when we have taken a last careful look down on to his back from behind, and observed the full spring of his ribs, with perhaps a reminiscent thought of the days when we thought saddles a stupid and unnecessary invention of parents and head-grooms, and loved rather to grip a living rib with a sympathetic knee, we may reasonably assume that we have found in that well-sprung rib the final necessary ingredient of true symmetry.

But some of you will say : " Padre, you old fraud, you have merely sketched all the points of a good terrier, and called the whole kerboodle ' symmetry ' ! " Kamerad, I own up, it is so ; but the emphasis in your protest must be laid upon *sketched*. That delicate adjustment of the whole body, fitly joined together and compacted by that which every joint helps to supply, each part working effectually together with the whole—that is symmetry. And if you think this rather a wordy definition of something that you really understand better yourself, sit down quickly and write your description of it, that it may be recorded, or ever you come to die !

VESUVIAN, by Ch. Splinter

CH. VENIO, by Vesuvian.

CHAPTER III.

Systematic Breeding.

The breeding of all stock is being largely influenced by our new knowledge of the laws of heredity, but none more than that of fox-terriers, because their breeding is very largely in the hands of men and women who have both the education and the leisure to keep themselves abreast with the recent revelations of scientists. No short cut to the findings of such knowledge can be obtained; but for a serious student, Eugene Davenport's " Principles of Breeding " (Ginn & Co.) is a very excellent work to begin upon. A cheaper little book, " The Theory and Practice of Breeding to Type, and Its Application to the Breeding of Dogs," by C. J. Davies ("Our Dogs," Manchester), is a good non-technical brochure.

Everyday science is throwing increasing light upon the bearing of heredity upon all live stock, and its application to the breeding of fox-terriers is likely to be very far-reaching in ts effects. This does not, however, render the old knowledge effete, as is often supposed, but the new knowledge of breeding applied to the pedigrees of fox-terriers will pave the way to fresh avenues of ever-increasing light, which will largely facilitate the progress of the breed.

The system now suggested emphasises the importance of the female line in each generation in what is called " tail female " (*i.e.*, dam's dam's dam, etc.), and in a less degree of the male line (sire's sire's sire, etc.), or " tail male." All other elements of a pedigree—that is, the middle lines leading back to the sire's dam's and the dam's sire's ancestors—are considered to be relatively less important as, in a sense, they cancel one another and may be largely ignored.

Thus a pedigree is now asserted to be in this proportion of importance:—

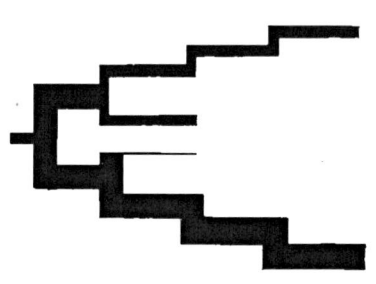

New proportion of values.

and not, as used to be thought, in this:—

Old proportion of values.

The varying thickness of these lines indicates relative importance.

The study of the breeding of modern fox-terriers can be reasonably developed on the same lines as have already proved of such immense help in the production, not of thoroughbreds and prize cattle only, but of all sorts of stock, in which scientific selection has been consistently practised since new facts became recognised.

What is here provided is a plan for the practical guidance of actual breeders, and not a logical or scientific theory; and our plan can be upset easily enough if, for instance, all the inside of the pedigree was made up of strains of Family 2, while the tail female alone was Family 1, for then the progeny would be called Family 1, while in essence, and cumulatively, it would owe more to Family 2; but unless that is striven for and arranged, it does not often happen in practical breeding, and the discounting of the middle pedigree, as cancelling itself out, proves, on the average, a sound policy.

Visto, by Ch. Venio.

Dark Blue, by Eton Blue, by Vibo, by Visto.

A scientist's answer to such a question as " Which is the most important parent ? " would necessarily be conditional and non-committal. To the student each of the nine qualities, which go to constitute a perfect terrier, must be approached separately ; and the influence of each parent depends upon its individual inherited dominance in that particular, and if both parents are potential in a different direction—or, more technically, the one dominant and the other recessive—the progeny will be divided on that point, irrespective of the parent's sex ; and this again is complicated by the fact that some qualities seem to be affected by the one sex, some by the other, and others again by each in alternate generations. Even if the dam is a more potential factor than the sire, with excellence so pronounced and competition so keen as is the case with fox-terriers, there cannot now be anything to give away on either side, so that practically there is little gained, even if the fact were established. At any rate we must discard the old fallacy that by picking up a decent and well-bred bitch, and mating her to an excellent sire, we have a reasonable chance of getting the very best. Breed only from good dams, bred from very good tails female.

It is quite a hopeless blunder to suppose that by breeding an ordinary bitch to an almost perfect stud dog progeny will result which, when bred together, will produce (according to the familiar formula) one almost perfect, two half-and-half, and one ordinary offspring among every four. Nothing of the sort will happen ; instead, unless a "million-to-one-against" fluke occurs, all will be sadly ordinary, because the formula does not apply to the mass of those separate characteristics, which make a perfect terrier collectively, but to his points separately.

FOX-TERRIER POINTS.

Now for those separate characteristics. We must look to our Fox-terrier Club standard, which (in spite of a grammatical " howler " and a solecism or two) is a very remarkable and thoughtful digest, responsible for our sound guidance already over some fifty years, and still as good as a new one is likely to be. The standard emphasises nine points (which sounds like a temperance reform programme), and these are :

(1) Head and ears ; (2) neck ; (3) shoulders and chest ; (4) back and loin ; (5) hindquarters ; (6) stern ; (7) legs and feet ; (8) coat ; and (9) symmetry, size, and character. Very well ! Now, could that plan be improved upon ? If, for instance (1) head was relegated to a less conspicuous position by being coupled with (2) neck, or if it were promoted to greater prominence by making a separate characteristic of eyes or of cheek, or of foreface, or of teeth, or by dividing it and making ears separate, is it not very probable that it might prove, after all, a mistaken correction ?

Suppose, then, the perfect smooth fox-terrier is one that has these nine points at their fullest and best, and suppose, for convenience, we refer to them by a single letter, thus :—

(1) H = Head and ears.
(2) N = Neck.
(3) S = Shoulders and chest.
(4) R = Back and loin—or ribs.
(5) Q = Hindquarters.
(6) T = Stern—or tail.
(7) L = Legs and feet.
(8) C = Coat.
(9) A = Activity—that is, symmetry, size, and character.

It proves necessary to introduce a new initial, as S means shoulder, and Ch might be misleading, perhaps, as standing for champion ; I have chosen *activity*, as the word active occurs in the standard in this connection, and in its best and fullest sense it will be a measure of symmetry of character and even of size.

Now, then, we get a perfect terrier technically described as :—

H . N . S . R . Q . T . L . C . A .

(It is open to any enthusiast to register his promising five-months' pup by this name, and it will hardly be more puzzling than, say, Physiostignim or Topolobompo, two distinguished terriers !)

The expert has now to reduce the qualities they represent into groups, if he can reasonably do so ; thus H (head) must probably stand alone, but N (neck) and S (shoulder) might combine, perhaps, as a really good neck will seldom fit into a

Ch. Oxonian, by Dark Blue, born 1902.

Ch. Orkney, by Ch. Oxonian.

bad shoulder, or vice-versa; so let S stand for neck and shoulders and chest. R (ribs) must probably stand alone, but Q (hindquarters) may well include T (stern or tail), as it is seldom we find a persistently faulty stern on ideal quarters, and the mere presence of the kink of a squirrel tail (though very unsightly) can hardly constitute an *essential* fault. L (legs and feet) and C (coat) cannot, of course, be considered as coupled characteristics, and even A (activity), since it includes size, cannot be regarded under S (shoulders), or Q (hindquarters), though closely related to both.

So we get the breeding aims reduced to :—
H . S . R . Q . L . C . A,
seven definite objects, and if a single breeder were lucky enough to establish a line of pure dominants in each of these qualities in, say, three generations, it would have taken the period between Grove Tartar, bred about 1859, and Ch. Myrtus, born in 1919, that is 60 years, to achieve the feat, for these two terriers are but 21 generations apart ; but, fortunately, the improvements can run concurrently, and that is what has happened. H has been, for instance, Nottingham's forte, S Hampshire's, R and Q have been strong in the Midlands, L in London, C in Wales, and A has claimed all districts ; and all have shared the successes of each.

Now the practical Mendelian must consider which of these points he is going to tackle most urgently ; he can quickly discover if he is dealing with a dominant or a recessive merit, and if he breeds loyally to the formula he can easily fail to breed a 100-guinea challenge cup winner, but can hardly fail to leave a footprint on the sands of terrierdom.

Of the seven points, it may be said that the good is generally recessive, thus :—

H Coarse heads are dominant over lean ones.
S Straight shoulders are dominant over sloping.
R Long backs and slack loins are dominant over short, well-ribbed bodies.
Q Weak crooked hindquarters are dominant over good ones.
L Bent legs and long thin feet are dominant over straight legs and round feet.

C Long soft coats are dominant over straight hard smooth coats.

A Here the order is the same ; good symmetry, average size, and vigorous activity of character are dominant over their opposites.

"Show me the best dog you can produce, and I will show three faults in him," frequently says one of our most successful breeders ; and he is right, for, profane as it may sound, even the immortal smooths, great terriers, as they were, have all had something very short of perfection, one, two, or perhaps three of their seven points. Think of them : Splinter's head, Result's feet, Raby Galliard's coat, Venio's second thigh, Dukedom's quarters, Oxonian's size, Levenside Luke's profile, Captain Double's underjaw, and it would hardly be nice to prolong it, but neither Darrell nor Kinver, nor even Myrtus, not to mention those still on the show bench, are free from a fault or two, plain and easy to see. Once, and only once, have I seen a smooth fox-terrier that I would not have dared to model afresh, and he had two faults ; one, that he was not mine—which was remedied ; and the other, that he died young—which was not. His third fault is that up to the present he has not risen again. Here's hoping !

The simplest Mendelian formula is this :—

Let H stand for a good-headed terrier.
,, B ,, ,, bad-headed one.

Breed H with B thus : ————————> H = B

The result will be an H and B blend thus : HB = HB
Then interbreed these crosses, and the result will be in the proportion of 1 pure H, 2 crossed H B, and 1 pure B in every 4 thus : ————————> H HB HB B
but the 2 H B crosses will have bad heads, as bad heads are dominant. Now the 1 out of 4, which is marked H, is a pure recessive, and he will beget only good heads, if mated to another pure H. It sounds quite easy ! But, then, H is only one of seven points, and the case of one point is complicated by what mathematicians call geometrical progression and concomitant

Ch. ORKADIAN, by Ch. Orkney.

variations, until it works out that, for every three million times that you would deal yourself thirteen trumps, you would breed one perfect fox-terrier, if you expected to breed him *by chance* !

SUCCESSFUL APPLICATION.

Dr. Master's success as a breeder is a very remarkable feature in recent fox-terrier history : to produce Ch. Wrose Indelible, Ch. Myrtus, Ch. Dunsting, Ch. Mint, and Ch. Cromwell Miss Legacy, could hardly be mere luck, nor was it so. The expert of Bury St. Edmunds is a typical example of the frequent success of persistent breeding, with the two essential ingredients—blood and brains ! How long he has been breeding smooths I cannot say, but the writer first became familiar with his name some twenty-five years ago, when he was already possessed of a Family 3 bitch called Coupon, from which he bred (by Ch. Oxonian) a young dog which he showed at the Crystal Palace in 1908, when he was second in a class of sixteen, under Mr. Redmond. Soon after, if not at the show, the dog was sold to Mrs. Losco Bradley at a price not exorbitant. Memory, like rumour, is often a lying jade, but I believe it was for £28. Anyhow, the dog did well, and finally emerged as Ch. Monkshood. In the same litter was a bitch, Flounce, and out of the same dam (Coupon) was another bitch (Skell), whom the far-seeing doctor mated to the best stud dog of the same family, Ch. King's Shilling (who was out of Princess Florizel, sister to Geisha, dam of Coupon : have you got it ?). Now, watch what happened. Skell's daughter by her kinsman bred Mayweed, and Flounce (Skell's sister) bred Milkweed, and Mayweed's daughter, Mayblossom, was mated to Milkweed's son, Mallow, so that the resulting daughter, Modesty, was as inbred on the female side to Family 3 as discretion dictated, and the doctor then did the right thing by outcrossing to a remote female family (7) in the person of Ch. Levenside Luke. The result would ordinarily be, in every family of four puppies, one pure 3, one pure 7 (probably in this case worthless), and two of blended or impure qualities, though perhaps good show terriers. There can be little doubt that two of the progeny, Malva and Martynia, were not only in name but in fact pure dominants of Family 3, though they would be regarded by the unobservant as being chiefly valuable as daughters of Ch. Levenside Luke, which was probably an event unimportant except as not eliminating the value of their dominance by the admixture of a powerful strain —that is, Luke's influence was effectively neutral.

It is at this point that an uncertain element must intervene. In Martynia and Malva the doctor had a concentrated essence of Family 3, tested by their resemblance to their maternal forbears, and he cast round for a sire for them of such general excellence and prepotency that his influence could be relied upon not to detract from the intrinsic qualities of the dam's strain, to which he had pinned his confidence, and yet of a line as distinct from their sire (who was " Jr.") as possible. Lest the sire's qualities should combine to work against the Family 3 inbred excellence, he chose a " So " sire (almost his only choice) in Cromwell Ochre's Legacy, and bred Ch. Myrtus, Ch. Wrose Indelible, Ch. Cromwell Miss Legacy, Ch. Dunsting, and Myosotis. And the casual onlooker merely murmurs : " Bit o' luck, what ? " But the doctor winks (metaphorically, of course), for his master-mind remembers Coupon in 1907. We must throw our bread upon the waters, as the doctor threw his Coupon, for he found it after many days !

Ch. Cromwell Ochre, "the glory dog,"
by Ch. Orkadian.

CHAPTER IV.

Lines and Families.

THE METHOD EXPLAINED.

The scientific system of breeding dogs on the same lines as thoroughbreds, cattle, and pigs, along lines and families, has been curiously neglected until recently in England, except among a few breeds, such as greyhounds and bassets. But there are constant signs that smooth fox-terrier men, at least, are awaking to the value of the secrets of success, which up to the present only a few realise, and fewer still practise. Such a sign comes to hand in a stud card (drawn up by that genuine student of method in breeding, Mr. Nigel Burke), on which the merits of a young dog are being urged, and which concludes by stating at length that he " traces his descent in tail male through a long line of champions to Ch. Splinter, the dominant line, and in tail female through Stardens Conceit and Rosamond to Vick (born 1872), by White Sam." But a time is coming when all that is contained in these lines will be summarised in the significant addition, " So 6," and all knowing breeders will then recognise the Splinter-Oxonian *line*, and will know that by belonging to *Family* 6 he is of the same strain as such bitches as Ch. Meifod Molly and her sister, Ch. Meifod Nelly, Ch. South Cave Siren, Ch. Haydon Dark Ruby, and the dams of Ch. Rowton Knight and old Dusky Diver—information which even the fullest pedigree would never reveal.

Our method is to denote the origin of each individual terrier by making clear the male tap-root from which his father's sire's sire's sire (right back) originally sprang by *letters*. These letters are followed by a *figure*, which shows how his mother's dam's dam's dam (also right back) is descended. Thus, Ch. Kinver is Jr 4. The letters refer to his tail male, for his sire is descended on the male side from Belvoir Joe (J) through Ch. Result (r), and the figure shows his tail female, for his dam is descended on the female side from White Fairy I, whelped in 1869, who is the founder of Family 4.

The male descent is known as the "Line," shown by the letters ; the female descent is called the "Family," and is shown by the figure.

In the lines, therefore, only dogs' names occur, and in families only bitches'. The only exception is that when a dog is a sire of a champion bitch, that bitch's name occurs to his credit in line ; and when a bitch is dam of a champion dog his name similarly occurs in her family.

The common principles of breeding are now reduced to scientific methods, and an inner circle of expert breeders of every variety of beast and bird follow the demands of this system. It is to that small and successful nucleus that the great body of fanciers owes the general excellence and progress of their stock. The accepted facts are now codified in general terms, and each particular variety of beast or bird benefits in a greater or less degree according to the number of its devotees who trouble to study the science, and according to the zeal and courage with which they apply it to their matings. At the same time, it must be said, on the other hand, that no amount of mere study, or zeal and courage in its application, will prove effective without the gift, natural or acquired, of *seeing* points, resemblances, and variations in the animals themselves. One outstanding principle is coming to be recognised in all modern systematic breeding, whether of thoroughbreds, Shorthorns, Leicesters, Large Blacks, Light Sussex, Dutch, Crests, or Selfs—I mean, of horses, cattle, sheep, pigs, poultry, rabbits, canaries, or even mice ;—and, incidentally, the last "small deer" must not be despised, as, owing to their early maturity, four or five generations can be studied in a year, so that in five years we can by comparison be back to the period of Belgrave Joe and Grove Nettle in smooth fox-terriers.

The principle to which I refer is the paramount importance of identifying and tracing the female family on the female side throughout, not only as dominating constitution and temper, as was known of old, but as having altogether as much sway in the realm of general excellence as the male line on the male side, whose importance was formerly a sort of shibboleth, when breeders were content to get any pure-bred bitch mated to an eminent sire, and hoped to reproduce him. Now, in the breeding of smooth, the male lines are extremely limited, and

CROMWELL OCHRE'S LEGACY,
by Cromwell Ochre, see page 144.

CROMWELL RAW UMBER, by "C.O.L."

amount in all to only three lines. There seems to be a sort of fatality about the number three in lines, for all thoroughbreds trace their origin to three lines of the Darley Arabian, the Godolphin Arabian, and the Byerley Turk ; and in smooth fox-terriers, all originally traced from Old Jock, Old Trap, and Foiler, but the two former are extinct, and Foiler alone survives in the Splinter line, for there were but three generations between the two dogs. To-day all smooth terriers alive trace in the tail male from Splinter (S), or from Belgrave Joe (J), or from Dusky D'Orsay (T). Splinter's line comes almost entirely through Ch. Oxonian's blood (So) ; Belgrave Joe's line comes largely through Ch. Result (Jr), but also along another line through Ch. Dominie (Jd) ; Dusky D'Orsay's line is the result of a modern cross with a dominant wire line through Dusky Collar (wire), son of Ch. Collar of Notts, a scion of the great wire line which leads back to the patriarchal wire sire, Tip (T). A successful sire derives his excellence over his many brothers and half-brothers from a combination of certain qualities of the female families in his pedigree, which work out in Mendelian proportions, only one terrier in every four bred the same way being a pure dominant in the matter of any particular quality or group of qualities.

There are some twenty-four families (each tracing back to a separate original bitch) which have produced an outstandingly good terrier, and each of these *families* or female strains is known by a number, just as the male strain or *line* is known by the letters S, J, and T. The first duty of a scientific breeder is to know the family of each of his bitches, which is often quite difficult ; another and much easier point is to ascertain the line of any sire he uses to mate with his bitches. The value of his eye for a terrier comes in, in knowing which qualities prevail in the few successful families, and, after choosing a bitch to breed from, discerning where she is true and where untrue to her family features, and so being able to mate her to a dog whose family (that is, whose dam's family) has qualities which will tend to remedy her own defects in her progeny. This is another way of repeating the wise old saying : " To breed a great male, put to a great male the best strain of his dam ; to breed a great female, put to a great male the best strain of his sire *as well as of his dam."* Tetrarch was a greater sire of fillies than of colts, because he was inbred on both sides to strong good-female-producing families. The late Cromwell Raw Umber bred five bitch champions to one dog champion for a similar reason, though his sire produced as many good dogs as bitches, not being of the same dominant good-female-producing family.

The most certain way of producing a successful strain is to examine the dam's side of the pedigree of the sire whom you most desire to reproduce, and to put to him bitches inbred on the female's side to the best and most dominant family in his dam's pedigree. Intense quality and inbreeding on persistent but discerning lines run together. If by a coincidence a breeder hits off a happy " nick " with a bitch at the first attempt, it will probably also be his last success unless he has the prudence to outcross the dam at once to a sire of one of the two distinctly different lines of male blood, which sire, however, must have some of the best blood of the *family* of the previous sire. If he pursues this course he has the foundations of a great and lasting succession of improving terriers in his own hands, and he is already on the high road to success.

Mr. Croxton Smith, in a clever article in a London newspaper, refers to the persistent work of Mr. Bruce Lowe, Sir Everett Millais, Mr. Allison, and the present writer, as enthusiasts on the theory of line breeding, and concludes with a little challenge to the only survivor, to show his faith by his works. Fortunately, however, for the efficacy of the Bruce-Lowe theory, as applied to dog-breeding, it does not depend in any serious way upon the future efforts of the four or five bitches which constitute my own kennels, but upon the past efforts of all the breeders of thoroughbred dogs for the last fifty years, who have together unconsciously made about, say, a hundred thousand experiments every year, and it is upon these that we base our faith in the system. In my own case, it is founded not on the future results of Formoola's or Foxformee's immediate puppies, but upon Avon May's fifteen generations, Bradley Victoria's fourteen generations, Ytene II's thirteen generations, and Dulcie's twelve generations; which have produced, respectively, fourteen champions (such as Donna Fortuna and Mumtaz) for Family 1, nine champions (such as Duchess of Durham and Dusky Doris) for Family 2, sixteen champions (such as The Sylph and Cromwell Miss Legacy) for

KIDDER KAZAN, by Cromwell Raw Umber.

Family 3, and ten champions (such as Lyons Sting and Cromwell Dark Dorothy) for Family 4. The case no longer remains, as we believe, to be tested and proved, but, rather, merely to be stated and acclaimed. We do not base our present convictions upon the hopes of the future, but upon the facts of the past. Thanks to the careful chronicles of our elders, the system is deeply engraved as a success upon the history of every breed, upon which has been expended research sufficient to test the efficacy of its activity. I am bound to labour this point, as every veteran at any rate who hears or reads the outlines of our research, invariably hurls at us the challenge, " Out with your champions as proof of your theory," oblivious of the fact that, in smooth fox-terriers alone, they have themselves already during this century at least six score champions out of six tap-root bitches, as against twenty champions bred by chance out of the rest, namely, twenty other families of bitches. As Mr. Croxton Smith says : " The system cannot be appreciated in all its bearings without careful study, but it can be explained generally in a few words." I express it thus : " The secret of it all is that the dam's dam's dam's dam, etc., is the chief factor in a pedigree, and after that the sire's sire's sire's sire, etc."

CHAPTER V.

Lines of Sires.

When we come to the tail male or direct male ancestry, it is surprising to find that every smooth fox-terrier to-day traces back to two dogs who flourished as recently as the eighties. These are Belgrave Joe and Ch. Splinter, and with the exception of that very small number of smooth terriers who descend from the wire line of Old Tip through Ch. Cackler of Notts, every known terrier descends from the line of these two dogs.

Of the two, Belgrave Joe (by Belvoir Joe by Trimmer) is the ancestor of Line J, and Ch. Splinter (tracing back through Foiler to Grove Tartar) is the founder of Line S. All other smooth lines I believe to be extinct, which is in itself a very curious and arresting fact.

LINE J (Belgrave Joe).

The table of Line J reveals many remarkable points, such as the extinction of the strain of Stipendiary and his son, Ch. D'Orsay, an event almost incredible to those who remember the importance it achieved in its day; the leanness of Ch. Levenside Luke's strain, considering his great opportunities; the success of big Camp Watteau (son of the writer's even bigger Milner), and its eclipse; and the temporary vogue of Ch. Dandyford's progeny. The values of Ch. Dominie and Ch. Result are such distinct features of Line J that it is necessary to distinguish their descendants by an added small letter. Dogs descended from Result and from Dominie are alike J (as descended from Joe), but Result's stock are known as Jr (J for Joe and r for Result), while Dominie's line are Jd (J again for Joe and d for Dominie); thus, though Ch. Kinver is Jr, Ch. Darrell is Jd.

A typical stud dog of this line was the writer's Ch. Dandyford Jr. 2, and his extended pedigree is of general interest.

Of his one hundred and eighty registered pups, one—Ch. Kinver—is Champion, and six are parents of champions, and four others have won challenge certificates. Briefly, his chief sons are: (1) Ch. Kinver, Jr 4, sire of Ch. Albino, Jr 23, and Southbro Suitus (now Levenside Look); (2) Sir

CH. LITTLE ARISTOCRAT, by Kidder Karzan, born 1922

Julian, Jr 2 (chal.), sire of Flodden, Jr 2 (chal.) ; (3) Dandy Pat, Jr 2, sire of Ch. Wrose Fanfare, Jr 4, and Hassan (chal.) ; (4) Flourish, Jr 2 (dd), sire of Southbro Sunblaze (chal.) ; (5) Anslow Dandy, sire of Bolton Woods Drummer (chal.). And his chief daughters are : (1) Jessie, dam of Ch. Kingsdown Prince, Jd 1 ; (2) Heartbroken, dam of Ch. Vortigern, So 2, and Ch. Jilted, So 2 ; (3) Lesterlin Souvenir, dam of Ch. Lesterlin Gay, T 12 ; (4) Arden and Selecta Peeress (chal.) ; (5) Southbro Salextra (chal.). Ch. Dandyford was born on December 29th, 1913, being bred by Mr. G. T. Brumby, and died as the result of an accidental oversight on September 26th, 1919 ; his skull is in the Birmingham University Dental Museum. A dog of exceedingly high spirit and emphatic temper, he was a great pet in the household of his last owner, though he left a mark with his teeth, which, after twelve years, is still visible on the thumb which pens these lines.

LINE Jr.

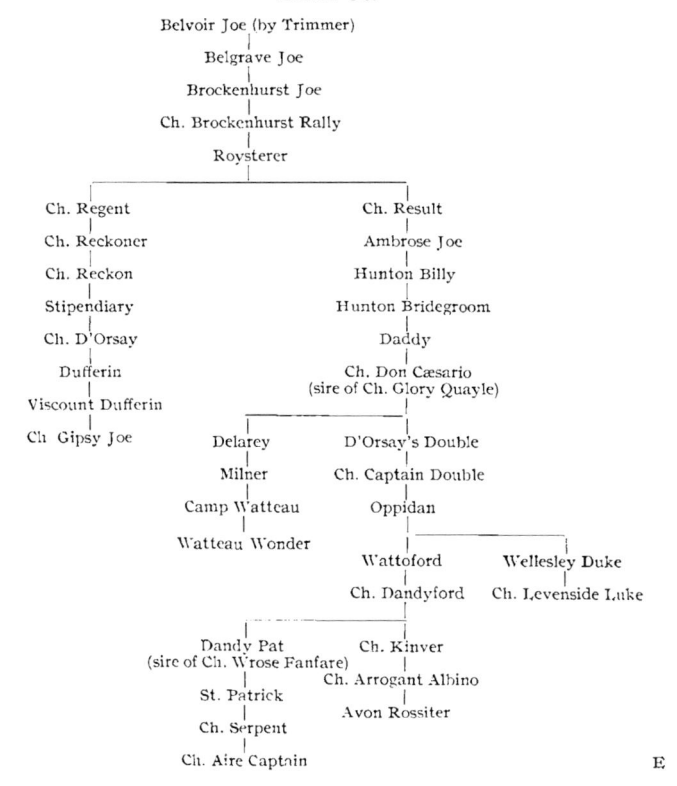

Belvoir Joe (by Trimmer)
Belgrave Joe
Brockenhurst Joe
Ch. Brockenhurst Rally
Roysterer

Ch. Regent
Ch. Reckoner
Ch. Reckon
Stipendiary
Ch. D'Orsay
Dufferin
Viscount Dufferin
Ch Gipsy Joe

Ch. Result
Ambrose Joe
Hunton Billy
Hunton Bridegroom
Daddy
Ch. Don Cæsario
(sire of Ch. Glory Quayle)

Delarey
Milner
Camp Watteau
Watteau Wonder

D'Orsay's Double
Ch. Captain Double
Oppidan
Wattoford
Ch. Dandyford

Wellesley Duke
Ch. Levenside Luke

Dandy Pat
(sire of Ch. Wrose Fanfare)
St. Patrick
Ch. Serpent
Ch. Aire Captain

Ch. Kinver
Ch. Arrogant Albino
Avon Rossiter

E

LINE Jd.

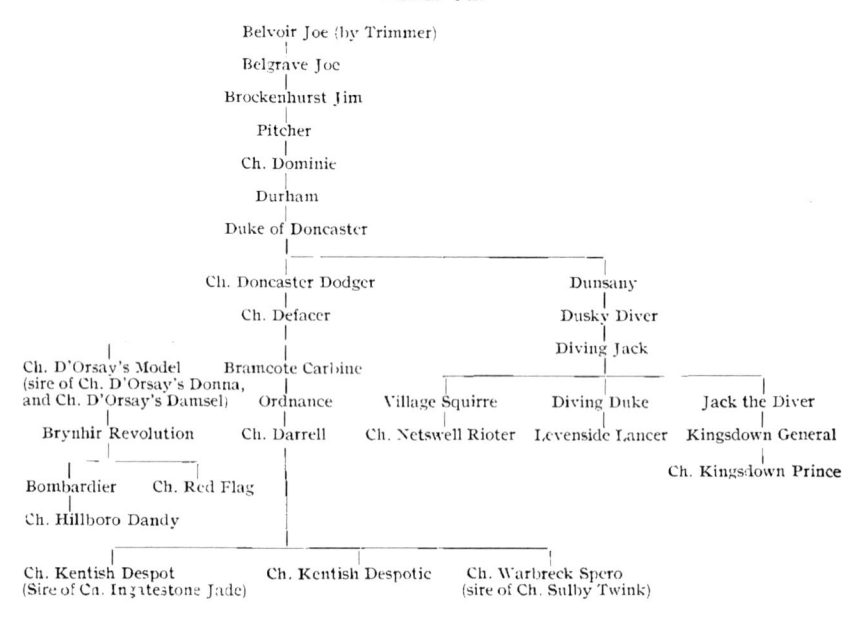

Belvoir Joe (by Trimmer)
|
Belgrave Joe
|
Brockenhurst Jim
|
Pitcher
|
Ch. Dominie
|
Durham
|
Duke of Doncaster
|
├───┐
Ch. Doncaster Dodger   Dunsany
| |
Ch. Defacer   Dusky Diver
| |
| Diving Jack
| |
Ch. D'Orsay's Model   Bramcote Carbine   ├──────────────────────┐
(sire of Ch. D'Orsay's Donna, | Diving Duke   Jack the Diver
and Ch. D'Orsay's Damsel)   Ordnance   Village Squirre | |
| | | Levenside Lancer   Kingsdown General
Brynhir Revolution   Ch. Darrell   Ch. Netswell Rioter |
| Ch. Kingsdown Prince
├──────────────┐
Bombardier   Ch. Red Flag
| |
Ch. Hillboro Dandy |
                     |
Ch. Kentish Despot   Ch. Kentish Despotic   Ch. Warbreck Spero
(Sire of Ch. Ingatestone Jade)   (sire of Ch. Sulby Twink)

Jr Wire Line.

Belgrave Joe
|
Brockenhurst Joe
|
Brockenhurst Jim
|
Pitcher
|
Ashton Trumps
|
Ashton Trumpeter
(Smooth, tracing back to Smooths)
|
Roper's Nutcracker
|
Barkby Co-respondent
|
Briar Sportsman
|
Alpha
|
Sylvan Rustic
|
Sylvan Reflex (w. 1907)
|
Ch. Brockley Gamester (w. 1909)
|
Ch. Last of Gamester

Ch. Selecta Ideal, by Ch. Little Aristocrat.

LINE S (including So).

CH. SPLINTER (by Dickon (16 lbs.), by Hognaston Dick, by Hognaston Willie (19 lbs.), by Old Foiler (17 lbs.), by Grip, by Grove Willie, by Grove Tartar)

- New Forest
  - Belmont Ranger
  - Despoiler (sire of Ch. Dame Fortune)
- Vesuvian (17 lbs.)
  - Ch. Venio (19 lbs.)
    - Visto
      - St. Leger (sire of Ch. Lorraine and Ch. Ridgewood Doris)
        - Ch. South Cave Leger
      - Viho
        - Étoui Bleu
        - Jack Blue (sire of Ch. Seven Trees Doris)
          - Sinopi
            - Ch. Ridgewood Re-echo
              - Ch. Ridgewood Reckon
                - Ruby Blue Cap
                - Ch. Detector
        - Ch. Oxonian (sire of Ch. Oxalis, Ch. Avon Music, and Ch. Rhodaford)
          - Ch. Avon Oxonhale
            - Ch. Tally-ho (sire of Ch. Tawdry)
              - Octavius (sire of Ch. Hotpa-lilt and Ch. Havoc)
                - Southboro' Sandman
                  - Ch. Brockford Dandy (sire of Ch. Watteau Nanette) and Ch. Udolon Dainty)
                - Morchard Cricketer
                  - Semloh Captain
                  - Ch. Semloh Superman
              - Ch. Sterling Surprise
                - Cromwell Desmond
                  - Ch. Chosen Don of Notts
                    - Legacy Lad
                    - Ch. Avon Mainstay (sire of Ch. Allista)
                      - Avon Myram (sire of Ch. Allista)
                    - Llandaff Peter of Delsmere (sire of Ch. Dunsefryad and Ch. Delsmere Dainty)
                      - Ch. Dunsmarvel
                - Ch. Adonis
          - Ch. Orkney
          - Ch. Orkadian (sire of Ch. Kitty Snarks and Ch. Misfit)
            - Ch. Cromwell Ochre
              - Cromwell Ochre's Legacy (sire of Ch. Cromwell Miss Legacy, Ch. Cromwell Dark Dorothy, Mint, Ch. Dunsting, and Ch. Hernon Bequest)
                - Ch. Blyino Topnote (dd)
                - Ch. That's Rippin' (dd)
                  - Sampler Marzipan
                    - Fern's Ideal (sire of Ch. Sampler Maymorn)
          - Cromwell Omera (sire of Ch. Aire Belle)
            - Dunifrico
            - Bowden Hamish
            - Ch. Bowden Bakish
        - The President
          - Billy Willan
            - Ch. Waterman (sire of Ch. Brynhir Bunty)
          - Ch. Monksbrood
          - Orkbie
        - Marcon
          - Dunbcayne
          - Ch. Dunkeath
          - Little Marcon
          - Tan (sire of Ch. Cromwell Tancgirl)
- Devastator
- Ch. Blizzard (b. 1898)
- Jack St. George
- Edstonian
- Fountainhead
- Bethel Dare Devil
- Dreadnought
  - Ch. Blytro Beggarman (dd)
    - Ch. Hernon Heir Apparent
  - Ch. Wrose Indelible (sire of Ch. Mumtaz)
  - Ch. Ryslip Re-echo
  - Cromwell Last of Umber
    - Ch. Cromwell Umber's Double
  - Ch. Charlton Autocrat
  - Ch. Paddock Premier
    - Cromwell Superb
      - Ch. Cromwell Superb's Replica (sire of Ch. Choicest Donna of Notts)
  - Ch. Swanpool Domino
  - Cromwell Raw Umber (dd) (sire of Ch. Cromwell Dark Girl, Ch. Cromwell Burnt Umber, Ch. Myrtia of Ovington, Ch. Heston Belle, Ch. Jillett, and Ch. Chosen Damsel of Notts)
  - Ch. Vortigern
  - Watteau Battleshaft
    - Ch. Farleton Flavian
  - Flambro
  - Kidder Karran (sire of Ch. Netsefol Radiance)
  - Ch. Little Aristocrat
  - Ch. Tara Belle (sire of Ch. Hernon Endowment, Ch. Hainworth Jess)
  - Ausus (sire of Ch. Kentish Effendina)

- Ch. Myrtis (dd) (sire of Ch. Dusky Dinah, Ch. Dusky Doris)
- Wool's Moor Dazzler
- Staunch Lad
- Ch. Staunch Steel
- Ark
- D'Orsay
- Ch. Dunetyle

- Ch. Delesmere Democrat
- Selecta Dictator
- Ch. Rikki Tikki Tavi
- Ch. Avon Sterling
- Ch. Selecta Ideal (sire of Ch. Selecta Melody)
- Ch. Selecta All Alone

LINE So (Splinter—Oxonian).

Splinter died of rabies in October, 1885, at an early age. Other pillars of this line are Despoiler (sire of Ch. Dame Fortune), Ch. Venio, Ch. Oxonian, and his grandson, Ch. Orkadian. Ch. Oxonian was a large, powerful dog, with good but imperfect feet ; he begat seven champions, and already thirty-five champions trace to him in tail male ; as he was born as recently as 1902, this is an amazing record, and one very difficult to equal. An " o " added after " S " denotes descent from Splinter through Oxonian.

Cromwell Ochre's Legacy long held the proud position of the sire of the greatest number of champions got by a smooth fox-terrier. For some time he shared with Ch. Oxonian the premier position as sire of seven, and although in grandchildren his ten made him superior to Ch. Oxonian's seven, he has surpassed his noble ancestor's long-held record with four champion sons, Ch. Myrtus, Ch. Blybro Top Note, Ch. Blybro Beggarman, and Ch. Wrose Indelible, and four daughters, Ch. Cromwell Miss Legacy, Ch. Dunsting, Ch. Cromwell Dark Dorothy, and Ch. Hermon Bequest. Here stood the proud record, challenging the prowess of terriers of the future to lower its colours ; as it did after nearly twenty years (for Ch. Oxonian was bred in 1902 by Mr. Desmond O'Connell, of course) at last surpass the record of success achieved by the mighty Oxonian, to be ultimately surpassed itself, as is shown later.

The S line arose in the Grove Hunt with Tartar and his son Willie, it reached eminence through Grip in the great Old Foiler, was then nearly lost, and saved by Parson O'Grady (Heaven rest his soul !), in Hognaston Willie and his son Dick, who sired Dickon, the father of Splinter (father and son being renowned for their perfect feet) and so on in direct male, through this amazing list of sires, Ch. Splinter, Vesuvian, Ch. Venio, Visto, Orkadian, Ch. Cromwell Ochre, Cromwell Ochre's Legacy, Ch. Blybro Top Note, Ch. Wrose Indelible, Ch. Little Aristocrat and Ch. Selecta Ideal, and the son of Cromwell Raw Umber, Ch. Vortigern. The list is a wonderful one, and a glance at it recalls the personality of a remarkable line of good sportsmen among their owners—Morgan, the old Grove huntsman ; Parsons Russell and O'Grady, Messrs. Luke Turner,

Redmond (who owned Dickon), Vicary, Tinne, Hack, O'Connell, Reeks, and Bradley ; as good an eleven of all-round sportsmen as a man could wish to succeed !

LINE T (Old Tip).

Line T from Old Tip is a wire-haired outcross, but it includes Dusky D'Orsay, the sire of Ch. Lesterlin Gay, and grandsire of Ch. Watteau Woodcock. The pillars are Meersbrook Bristles, Ch. Cackler of Notts, and Comedian of Notts. Cackler was sire of Dusky Cackler, who was g-g-g-g-grandsire of Dusky D'Orsay, whose stock may yet loom large in the production of good smooths, as an outcross to the only other lines.

An old-time fancier lately wrote, saying :—

" I think Mr. Redmond did breeders a good turn when he crossed his grand bitch [Ch. D'Orsay's Donna, of course] with the wire Dusky Collar."

Whatever is said about this step (and much was and even will be) that obstinate old cuss, " the fact," remains that some unquestionably good stock resulted, as the following skeleton diagram shows :—

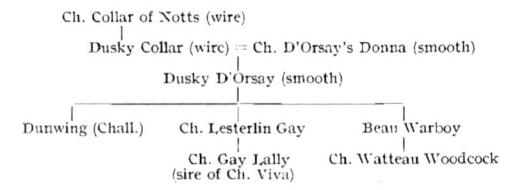

```
            Ch. Collar of Notts (wire)
                     |
            Dusky Collar (wire) = Ch. D'Orsay's Donna (smooth)
                     |
                Dusky D'Orsay (smooth)
    _____|_____
    |               |                |
Dunwing (Chall.)  Ch. Lesterlin Gay  Beau Warboy
                     |                |
                Ch. Gay Lally    Ch. Watteau Woodcock
                (sire of Ch. Viva)
```

Here is a beginning which, when the So line has blended so fully with the Jr and the Jd lines that a further outcross is necessary, will provide exactly what will then be essential. It may easily be that in another fifty years' time, all the last fifty years of triumphant successes in breeding and exhibiting which we all associate with the name of the present Chairman of the Committee of the Kennel Club, will be as the memory of other great lights of times past, and that the name of Mr. Francis Redmond will, to the next generation of systematic breeders, be synonymous with the plucky founder of line T, which saved the breed ! Probably the contemporaries of

Ch. Avon Sterling, by Ch. Selecta Ideal

Ch. Selecta All Alone, by Ch. Selecta Ideal

T

TIP (Kendal's kennel bred terrier)
Pincher
Old Jester
Young Jester (w. 1884)
Knavesmire Jest (w. 1885)
Ch. (U.S.) Meersbrook Bristles (w. 1892)

Broomhill Member   Meersbrook Ben
Royston Record   Ch. Barkley Ben, w. 1897
Royston Ringleader   Ch. Cackler of Notts (w. 1898)
Millgate Leader   Ch. Briar   Ch. Dusky   Ch. Dusky Cackler (w. 1900)
Briggate (w. 1906) Cackler   Cracker   Morden Blusterer (w. 1902)
Round Up   Catch 'em of Notts (w. 1904)
Ch. Drumlee Go Bang   Cornelian of Notts (w. 1906)

                                                              Ch. Collar of Notts (w. 1907)
Ch. Chunky of Notts (w. 1908)
Ch. Wireboy of Paignton (w. 1912)   Ch. Collarbone of Notts (w. 1909)   Corker of Notts (w. 1911)
                                     Wincanton Rufus   Barrington Cracker (w. 1911)
Ch. Deykin Wire Boy   Wyche Warrant   Briar Tetratema   Ch.   Watteau Warrior (w. 1915)   Consulter of Notts (w. 1917)   Barrington Fearnought
Ch. Speedy Ball   Gedling Tetrascamp Signal   Ch. Brakesmere Benedict   Ch. Wycollar Trail
Ch. Aman Fox Trot   Ch. Wyche Workman   Ch. Wyche Wallet   Iveshead Scamp   Wire   (w. 1917)   Crack o' the Trail   Ch. Cicero
                    Ch. Wyche Wrangler   Ch. Dan y Craig Bondman   Ch. Epping Emblem   Ch. Whitecroft Reflex
                    Brynhir Captain   Ch. Barrington Bridegroom
                    Brynhir Burner   Ch. Trevlac Tip Top   (w. 1919)
                    Ch. Thet Fusilier
                                                        Ch. Roboro Play Boy   Ch. Crackley Sensation   Ch. Wyche Warm   Ch. Barry B
                                                                                                        Ch. Cayenne of Carce   Gedling W
                                         Ch. Wycliff Warfare   Ch. Crackley Sensational   Ch. Epping Extreme   Ch. Bolton Woods Wonder   Warm Safe
                                         Ch. Cosford Crasher   Ch. Crackley Supreme   Ch. Kempshurst Consul   Ch. Gedling
                                         Ch. Bobby Burns of Wildoaks   Ch. Cornwell Cyclone   Nedwob H
                                                                                                                                          Ch. Nedwo

LINE.

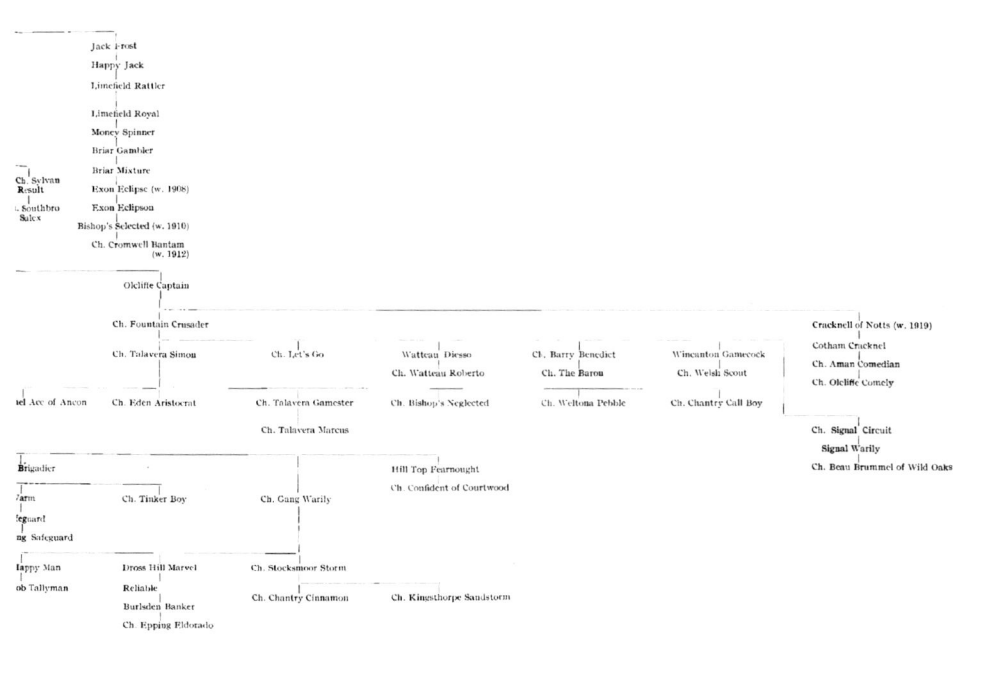

Jack Frost
Happy Jack
Limefield Rattler
Limefield Royal
Money Spinner
Briar Gambler
Briar Mixture
Ch. Sylvan Result — Exon Eclipse (w. 1908)
Southbro Salex — Exon Eclipson
Bishop's Selected (w. 1910)
Ch. Cromwell Bantam (w. 1912)

Olcliffe Captain

Ch. Fountain Crusader · Cracknell of Notts (w. 1919)
Cotham Cracknel
Ch. Talavera Simon · Ch. Let's Go · Watteau Diesso · Ch. Barry Benedict · Wincanton Gamecock · Ch. Aman Comedian
Ch. Watteau Roberto · Ch. The Baron · Ch. Welsh Scout · Ch. Olcliffe Comely

Ace of Ancon · Ch. Eden Aristocrat · Ch. Talavera Gamester · Ch. Bishop's Neglected · Ch. Weltona Pebble · Ch. Chantry Call Boy
Ch. Talavera Marcus · Ch. Signal Circuit
Signal Warily
Ch. Beau Brummel of Wild Oaks

Brigadier · Hill Top Fearnought
Farm · Ch. Tinker Boy · Ch. Gang Warily · Ch. Confident of Courtwood
Safeguard
ng Safeguard

Happy Man · Dross Hill Marvel · Ch. Stocksmoor Storm
ob Tallyman · Reliable
Burlsden Banker · Ch. Chantry Cinnamon · Ch. Kingsthorpe Sandstorm
Ch. Epping Eldorado

Cleopatra never worried much about her needle, nor those of Sir Walter Raleigh about his muddy blazer (carefully, please, printer !) ; perhaps even Lady Whittington was ignorant as to her Dick's cat when once the Lord Mayor had " relinquished the fancy " ! So we are overlooking, it may be, the outstanding importance of our great third string in readiness for the future of smooth fox-terriers. Time alone will tell.

So far the three champions are the result of T.

Ch. Collar of Notts is descended thus :—

Old Tip, Pincher, Old Jester, Young Jester, Knavesmire Jest, Meersbrook Bristles, Meersbrook Ben, Ch. Barkby Ben, Ch. Cackler of Notts, Dusky Cackler, Morden Blusterer, Catch 'Em of Notts, Comedian of Notts, Ch. Collar of Notts.

CHAPTER VI.

Families of Dams.

Records of systematic breeding of modern fox-terriers can only be traced to about 1862, in which year the Rev. W. Handley bred a bitch called Sting, who became the dam of Grove Nettle. About the same time Lord Huntly bred Venom, the dam of Tricksey; and Parson Jack Russell produced a little later the rough-coated Juddy, who was the dam of Moss I. From these three "Eves" descend nearly all the terriers of to-day; indeed, if we add the name of one other bitch, White Fairy I, born about the same time, we have mentioned the direct female ancestors of nearly every notable smooth fox-terrier now alive.

There are, however, a few other contemporary bitches, as will be seen, yet to be included among the founders of good families in the past. Beyond these bitches it is difficult to trace any others that have been the direct female ancestors of more than one champion terrier, but of those who have even achieved this distinction there are about sixteen, making some twenty-four tap-roots or families in all, though many of these may be found to be extinct. The proportionate excellence of the first four great families is proved by a glance at the families of the many good champions alive at the moment; no other family has produced more than one.

FOUNDERS OF FAMILIES.

Parson Jack Russell's JUDDY, 1868 (through Avon May, 1887) ...	1
Lord Huntly's VENOM, 1866	2
The Rev. W. Handley's STING, 1861 (through Grove Nettle, 1862)	3
WHITE FAIRY I, 1869	4
PATCH, 1876 (through Barrowby Pearl)	5
VIC, 1872, by White Sam	6
GIP, 1877, dam of Nell IV, 1879 (through Avon Vesta)	7
RUSTIC QUEEN, 1884 (through Elmhurst Topsy, 1894)	8
SPOT, 1876, dam of Effie Deans (through Minting Queen) ...	9
GRANTHAM'S NETTLE, 1862 (through Broseley Saucy, 1886) ...	10

BELGRAVE JOE, the original J, by Belvoir Joe,
by Trimmer, ancestors of Jr and Jd lines.

CH. RESULT, the original Jr,
by Roysterer, by Ch. Brockenhurst.

PINK (of the Quorn Hunt), 1866	11
GRACE NEWCOME, 1898	12
OLD VICK, by Jock, 1876	13
BRANSON'S VIC, 1886	14
VIC, by Dudley Swindler, 1893	15
BURBIE, by Tweezer, 1877 (through Ch. Rant)	16
ROSE, dam of Ness Myrtle, 1882	17
JERSEY NELL	18
ARROWSMITH'S NETTLE, 1869...	19
PATRICA (Wire), 1898	20
FLORIST (Wire), 1898	21
LOVE LADY	22
VIC, by Ragman	23
PATTI, by Rattler	24
Untraced Origin	x

We have traced the pedigrees of most of the terriers who have become champions since January 1st, 1901, back to their founders. It is a remarkable fact that, owing to the great care spent in times past on the records of smooth terriers, a modern historian can— not, of course, without considerable research— classify practically every terrier that comes along as methodically as he could a thoroughbred. Inquiries often come as to how it can be done, and the answer is that access must be had to the Kennel Club Registry of every dog ever registered (the writer has a copy of this), and to the Fox-terrier Club stud books ; and when these fail the only hope for unregistered terriers is a large collection of contemporary stud cards, which, if they bear the name of a responsible breeder, may be taken as pretty good evidence. As a last resort, one is perhaps driven to appeal to old-time fanciers, whose fifty-year-old records are generally most courteously made available. There are numbers of educated fanciers, who still are unconverted to the lines and families system, and who adhere to the old plan of equal values of all ancestors, but generally they prove on closer examination to be unbelievers in scientific heredity altogether, and to pin their faith very largely to chance ; and, to be frank, so good so pure so choice are the smooth fox-terrier lines and families that, if men merely sow their seed in the furrows of more exact students, they will very often reap plenteously, breeding as it were on the brains of others, as a parasite lives on the blood of his host.

FAMILY 1.

Family 1 is descended in the tail female from Moss I, who was born about 1869, the daughter of Parson Russell's old bitch Juddy, commonly known as Judy. The family soon acquired celebrity, as Moss II (ex Moss I) whelped the great Ch. Brockenhurst Rally, who besides siring Ch. Raffle, was grand-grandsire of Ch. Result and Regent, pillars of Line J.

The question of " Jack Russell " terriers seems to have a peculiar interest, and it is worthy of note that, though all smooth fox-terriers descend from the old sporting parson's strain, only certain ones descend from it in direct female succession. They are known as Family 1, which includes some of the very best terriers that have ever lived ; but latterly it has not been so prominent as a few years ago. It began with the Rev. J. Russell's Juddy (dam of Moss I, dam of Frolic, whose strain ran down to the dam of Ch. Tallyho), of Moss II (dam of Ch. Brockenhurst Rally), and Moss I (dam of Frantic), was g-g-grand-dam of the pivot bitch Avon May, from whom sprang, among others, through a string of Mr. Locke Lancaster's " Camp " bitches, Darrell's Dame, who was dam of Karswood, Dark Model, Dunstable Splinter, and Lady Claudia, who whelped Dunstable Prince and Princess. Every terrier, therefore, of Family 1 is a pure Jack Russell terrier. It is a family so good so sound and so sporting, that it is almost certain to survive as a permanent root. We are awaiting another Donna Fortuna among her progeny, and some of us never see a new-born puppy of this family, with a pure white body and two little wee black ears, without a shimmer of reminiscent excitement and a desire to speculate the traditional " fiver." Here's to the great unborn !

Blybro Mischief, the dam of Top Note and many another sound terrier, traces to Donation in three generations of her tail female. Now, Donation was a very stout, well-ribbed, characteristic brood bitch, a litter sister to Ch. Avon Music, Burton Nellie (dam of Ch. Defacer), and Elton Mixture. This excellent litter was by Ch. Oxonian ex Victorious, who traces in three generations to Avon May, and in six more to Juddy, Jack Russell's terrier, who founded Family 1. The survival of Donation in her progeny is very illuminating, for besides being stout and well-ribbed, this heavily-marked little bitch had

D'Orsay's Double, Jr.

Ch. Capt. Double, Jr. by D'Orsay's Double.
"The Glory of Northumberland," born 1902.

F.

Parson Jack Russell's **JUDDY** (or Ju

Moss I.

Frolic (a)		Frantic (a)
Brockenhurst Frolic		Frenzy
Judith		Vashti II.
Jingle II.		Mayfield Vic
Chimes		Avon May, b. 1
Dirge	Donna Dominie	Dominissa
Paith Prim	Dusky Diva	Directress
Terrible Calamity		
Take Care	Dareen	Dame D'Orsay
Tariff (dam of Ch. Tally-ho)	Court Beauty (dam of Ch. Dangler)	Cherry B. (dam of Ch. Captain Double)	Ch. Dame Fortu
			Ch. Donna Fort
			Donna Rosa
		Camp Winnie	Donna Ves
		Camp Water	Donna Viol
Lady Graduate	Camp White Woman	Camp Waterlily (dam of Camp Watteau)	Duchess of Par
Townsend White Tip			
Townsend Queenie	Camp Winning Woman	Camp Waxy	Tarolinta
Fox Earth Merrian	Darrell's Dame (dam of Dark Model)	Twiggle	Jill
(See **INCOMPLETE** under Family 24)	Lady Claudia	Twiddly Bit	Merriment (dam of Milner)
		Netley	
Dunstable Princess (dam of Kidder Kargan)	Barley Beauty	Jesse (dam of Ch. Kingsdown Prince)	
Selecta Decision	Netswell Roulette		
Ch. Selecta Melody		Ring Bridget	
		Ring Duchess (dam of Ch. Paddock Premier)	

FAMILY 1.

(udy), 1868.

|
Moss II
(dam of Ch. Brockenhurst Rally)

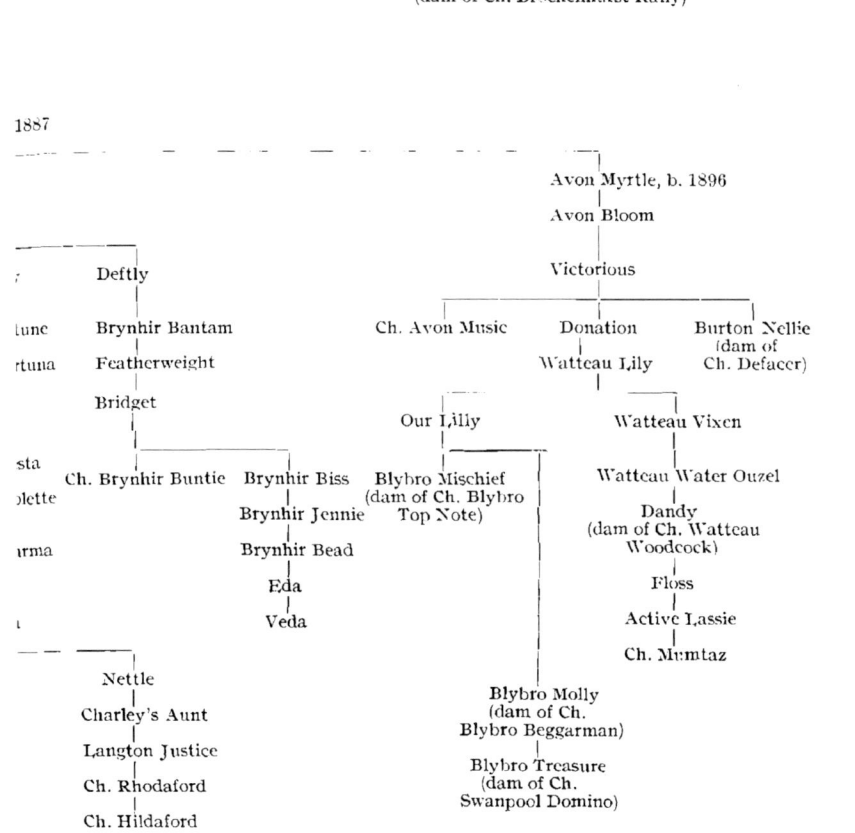

1887

Avon Myrtle, b. 1896
|
Avon Bloom
|
Victorious

Deftly
|
une   Brynhir Bantam   Ch. Avon Music   Donation   Burton Nellie
rtuna   Featherweight | (dam of
            | Watteau Lily   Ch. Defacer)
            Bridget |
sta | Watteau Vixen
            Ch. Brynhir Buntie Brynhir Biss   Blybro Mischief |
)lette | (dam of Ch. Blybro   Watteau Water Ouzel
                                Brynhir Jennie Top Note) |
                                    | Dandy
ırma   Brynhir Bead   (dam of Ch. Watteau
                                    | Woodcock)
                                Eda |
                                    | Floss
l   Veda |
                                                                     Active Lassie
                                                                     |
                                                                     Ch. Mumtaz
            Nettle   Blybro Molly
            | (dam of Ch.
            Charley's Aunt   Blybro Beggarman)
            | |
            Langton Justice   Blybro Treasure
            | (dam of Ch.
            Ch. Rhodaford   Swanpool Domino)
            |
            Ch. Hildaford

superlatively good bone and exquisite feet, and a more than fair head. Then, you will say, of course, she was an obvious brood bitch ; but no ! I attribute considerable credit to Mr. Calvert Butler for putting such confidence in a bitch which, with all her virtues, was short and cobby not only in back, but also in neck, and even a little strong in her long head, which the heavy black markings of head, neck, and shoulders did nothing to relieve.

About 1888, Mr. Francis Redmond acquired from Mr. Frank Reeks a bitch of great merit, named Avon May, who became an important matron of this family, which reached a very great position when Ch. Dame Fortune and her peerless daughter, Ch. Donna Fortuna, flourished. Fortunately, they have left us progeny. This family has also produced Ch. Brynhir Buntie, Ch. Rhodaford, Ch. Hildaford, Camp Waterlily, Ch. Mumtaz, Ch. Selecta Melody, and the dams of Ch. Tallyho, Ch. Defacer, Ch. Captain Double, Ch. Watteau Woodcock, Ch. Blybro Top Note, Ch. Blybro Beggarman, Ch. Paddock Premier, and Ch. Swanpool Domino.

There is a curious point to be observed in this family, which may illustrate an important principle. At the tenth generation from their common founder, Juddy, no less than six bitches, descending on different lines, produced these remarkable puppies, Ch. Captain Double, Ch. Donna Fortuna, Ch. Defacer, Ch. Avon Music, Ch. Tallyho, and Ch. Dangler; and, as the dam of Ch. Donna Fortuna, Ch. Dame Fortune, was also alive, there could at that time be little question as to this being the premier family, an honour which, twenty years later, might certainly be challenged. Now, students have to discover some sort of a common type (derived from Avon May and her tail female), which shows itself in the merits and defects of these six typical Family 1 terriers, and it proves the more interesting in that none of them are by the same sire. Their heads, both in length and quality, are clearly beyond serious cavil ; but, if in a family the skull, which in a sense is the last and most developed of the cervical vertebræ, is almost unfailingly long and lean, it is almost inevitable that the other vertebræ will also have a similar length, so that a lean-headed terrier seldom or never has a short, stumpy neck—even if his shoulder is so badly adjusted that he appears to have ; but with the neck joints so fixedly long it is not probable that their neighbours further along may have a sympathetic tendency? Enough—or some shrewd critic will emphatically assert that Family 1 terriers tend to have long backs, and every owner of such terriers will either believe it and want to get rid of his Family 1 terriers, or disbelieve it and want to bestow umpteen strokes with the animal which has just been so rashly let out of the bag! One word more; if it appears that a certain family has a leaning towards long backs, or any other fault, let no breeder hope to eradicate that trait by mating a bitch to a terrier with too short a back—and a back can easily be too short, though most novices will not believe it, or even understand it—for if one parent has a faulty body in one way, and the other parent also a faulty body even in an opposite way, the chances are thousands to one against a good body resulting, for neither parent has it, and opposite faults never blend into a virtue. To eradicate a fault, breed with a male who is perfect, but not exaggerated, in the faulty feature.

Twenty champions are so far of Family 1.

FAMILY 2.

Family 2 originated about 1866, with Lord Huntly's Venom, whose granddaughter, Diamond, won a second prize at Birmingham in 1870. From her sprang a family as conspicuous as Family 1 for general excellence and for the number of representative bitches it produces. Family 2 claims:—

Ch. Brockenhurst Dainty II, Ch. Brockenhurst Lottery, Ch. Vesuvienne, Ch. Duchess of Durham, Ch. Cymru Queen, Ch. Help-a-bit, Ch. Havoc, Ch. Jilted, Ch. Dusky Doris, Ch. Viva, Ch. Hermon Bequest, Ch. Hermon Endowment, Ch. Kentish Effendina, Ch. Sampler Maymorn, and Ch. Raine Rarity.

It also claims the dams of:—

Sir Julian, Ch. Adonis, Ch. Dandyford, Ch. Netswell Rioter, Ch. Valuator, Ch. Orkney, Ch. Dunleath, Ch. Venio, Ch. D'Orsay's Model, Ch. Drusus, Ch. Avon Oxendale, Ch. Oxonian, his sire Dark Blue, Ch. Vortigern, Ch. Hermon Heir Apparent, Ch. Hillboro Dandy, Ch. Serpent, and Ch. Bowden Rakish.

Ch. Raby Galliard, born 1903

Ch. Dandyford, the war-time Ch. sire.

FAMILY 2.

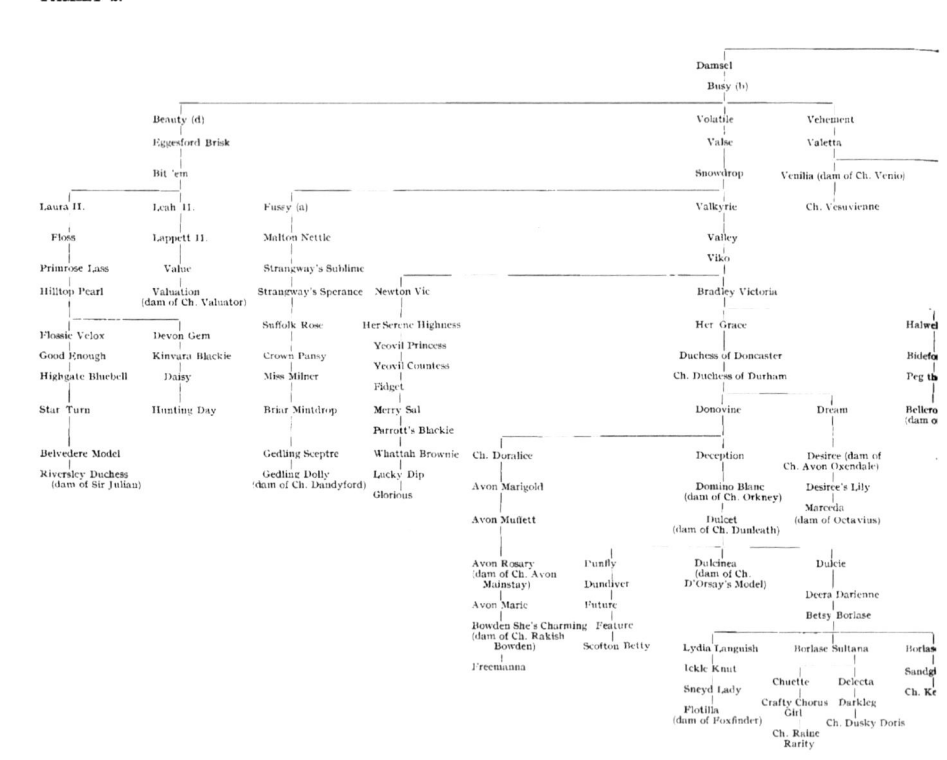

```
                                                                                            Damsel
                                                                                            Busy (b)
                                              ┌─────────────────────────────────────────────────┴────────────────┐
                                         Beauty (d)                                    Volatile              Vehement
                                              │                                           │                     │
                                     Eggesford Brisk                                    Valse                Valetta
                                              │                                           │                     │
                                          Bit 'em                                      Snowdrop       Venilia (dam of Ch. Venio)
          ┌────────────┬──────────────────────┴────────────────┐                          │                     │
      Laura II.     Leah II.                Fusey (a)                                  Valkyrie           Ch. Vesuvienne
          │            │                        │                                         │
       Floss       Lappett II.            Malton Nettle                                 Valley
          │            │                        │                                         │
    Primrose Lass    Value              Strangway's Sublime                              Viko
          │            │              ┌─────────┴─────────┐                               │
    Hilltop Pearl  Valuation   Strangway's Sperance  Newton Vic                    Bradley Victoria
                 (dam of Ch. Valuator)      │               │
        ┌──────────┐         ┌──────────────┤       ┌───────┴──────────┐             ┌────┴─────────┐                       ┌──
   Flossie Velox  Devon Gem  Suffolk Rose   │  Her Serene Highness    │          Her Grace                                Halwel
        │            │            │         │       Yeovil Princess                    │
   Good Enough  Kinvara Blackie  Crown Pansy│               │                  Duchess of Doncaster                      Bidefo
        │            │            │         │       Yeovil Countess                    │
   Highgate Bluebell Daisy    Miss Milner   │           Fidget                 Ch. Duchess of Durham                     Peg th
        │            │            │         │
    Star Turn   Hunting Day   Briar Mintdrop│        Merry Sal                      Donovine              Dream          Bellero
        │                         │         │     Parrott's Blackie                     │                   │           (dam o
  Belvedere Model            Gedling Sceptre│    Whattah Brownie   Ch. Doralice     Deception         Desiree (dam of
        │                         │         │           │                │               │          Ch. Avon Oxendale)
 Riversley Duchess         Gedling Dolly    │       Lucky Dip       Avon Marigold   Domino Blanc       Desiree's Lily
  (dam of Sir Julian)    (dam of Ch. Dandyford)│       Glorious           │         (dam of Ch. Orkney)       │
                                              │                      Avon Mullett          │              Marceda
                                              │                                          Dulcet       (dam of Octavius)
                                              │                                    (dam of Ch. Dunleath)
                                              │                     ┌───────────┐        │
                                              │              Avon Rosary     Punfly   Dulcinea              Dulcie
                                              │           (dam of Ch. Avon     │     (dam of Ch.              │
                                              │              Mainstay)     Dandiver   D'Orsay's Model)   Deera Darienne
                                              │                  │             │                             │
                                              │             Avon Marie      Future                       Betsy Borlase
                                              │         ┌────────┴────────┐
                                              │    Bowden She's Charming  Feature
                                              │   (dam of Ch. Rakish        │
                                              │        Bowden)           Scofton Betty    Lydia Languish    Borlase Sultana      Borlas
                                              │          │                                      │                                Sandg
                                              │      Freemanna                              Ickle Knut            ┌────┬─────┐   Ch. Ke
                                              │                                                  │             Chuette Delecta
                                              │                                              Sneyd Lady           │      │
                                              │                                                  │         Crafty Chorus Darkleg
                                              │                                              Flotilla           Girl
                                              │                                          (dam of Foxfinder)              Ch. Dusky Doris
                                              │                                                           Ch. Raine
                                              │                                                              Rarity
```

d Huntly's **VENOM**, b. 1866, "All white"—from Morgan, Huntsman of the
Grove Hounds, with whom she ran two seasons).
Tricksey (brown patch on side)
|
Diamond

		Daze	Dusty	
		Brockenhurst Dainty		
		Ch. Brockenhurst Dainty II.	Ch. Diamond Dust	Dust
		Ch. Brockenhurst Lottery	Deacon Diamond	Kohinoor	Brickdust
		Absence	Brockenhurst Gem	Splinter's Bar (Daylesford Splinteria)	Dirty
Varema	Verona		Auburn	Lady Sal	Barrowby Shifty
Velzie	Pembro Pearl	Struck Out	Doldrums	Northfida Sal	B'by Ramble
Blackcap	Pembro Jewel	Waif (dam of Dark Blue)		School Green Floss	B'by Defty
Helmet	Ch. Cymru Queen	Old Gold	Brockenhurst Margaret	Furnace Nettle	Barrowby Shining
Hospitality	Flame	Guinea Gold	Brockenhurst Dame	West End Rosebud	B'by Prude
Hardpushed	Flake	Charlton Guinea Gold	Dognes	Lobelia	Grace Newcombe (See F.T.F., Apl. 19th, 1929, and Family XII).
Death Struggle	Honey	Flutter	Overture (dam of Ch. Oxonian)	Mrs. Fry	Lucky Omen
Atropa	Sweet Morsel	Forethought		Okehurst Blue Stocking	Ch. Cocoatina of Notts
Herbalist	Bon Bouche	Foresight		Okehurst Patience	See **Family 2 - Wire**
	Hibernico	Flodden (Chall.)		Okehurst Venom	
Help-a-bit Ch. Havoc (dam of S. Patrick, sire of Ch. Serpent)	Pit-a-pat	Floodgate	Dusky Flo (Chall.)	Freehold Duchess (dam of Ch. Adonis)	
Margery		Fluid		Flagon	Typist
Ch. Hermon Bequest (dam of Ch. Hermon Heir Apparent)	Orelle	Dandy Duchess (dam of Ch. Gay Lally)	Heartbroken (dam of Ch. Vortigern)	Via	Manor Duchess
Hermon Dowry				Ch. Viva	Ch. Sampler
Ch. Hermon Endowment	Harmony	Avon Roulette	Ch. Jilted	Vee	Followdon Maymorn
		Avon Radne (dam of Netswell Rioter)		Last Chance (dam of Ch. Serpent)	
Joyeuse	Anemone (dam of Ch. Red Flag)	Minnehaha			
Ha-ha		Sweet Refrain (dam of Ch. Hillboro Dandy)			
Funnywee					

h Effendina

FAMILY 2—Wire.

WEST END ROSEBUD (See Family 2)

Lobelia
├── Lill
│   ├── Lady Victoria
│   ├── Wyville Queen
│   ├── Crystal Kitty
│   ├── Hilda
│   └── Gosford Lilian
│   (dam of Ch. Epping
│   Extreme and
│   Ch. Gosford Crasher)
├── Ch. Cocoatina of Notts
│   ├── Common Frump of Notts
│   ├── Ch. Chipped Tip of Notts
│   ├── Clipper of Notts
│   │   (dam of Ch. Roboro
│   │   Playboy)
│   ├── Dairy Maid
│   └── Idloes Swift Girl
│   (dam of
│   Ch. Aman Fox-trot)
└── Lucky Omen
    ├── Coffee of Notts
    ├── Treviac Tartlet
    ├── Ch. Eden Bridesmaid
    │   (dam of
    │   Ch. Crackley Supreme
    │   and
    │   Ch. Eden Aristocrat)
    └── Codded of Notts
        (dam of Ch. Common
        Scamp of Notts)

85

This family is at present well in the ascendant, and in a few years may establish a supremacy over all others, for it has become obvious that one good terrier may become the direct ancestor of nearly all living in a period of thirty years ; and though this is far easier for a dog than a bitch, the discovery of such a jewel as, say, Domino Blanc, might even still overwhelm all competition, just as Moss, Venom, and Sting did in the sixties, but she would have to be very prolific.

Now, what are the common points in Family 2 ? Are they short of heart-room, lacking in ample spring of rib ? Do they fail in substance, in straightness of limb, or in compactness of foot ? Have they even a shade of slackness in loin or quarter ? I think not. But why no mention of long lean lasting heads, small eyes, and smart fascinating ears ? And should the tail be carried in a line parallel with the front legs or at an angle of 45 degrees to them ? Well ! well ! You can very rarely have everything, and when you do get a Family II terrier with a good feature, which is not characteristic of the family, the strong probability is that she also fails to carry many guns in the family's usual merits.

It is the dream of the novice only to breed an alligatorial head upon a creature of elephantine bone and hippopotamean girth ; for though it might rank high as a typical representative of a duck-billed platypus, it would completely lack that grace and symmetry " which stamps the caste of " terriers !

Thirty-four champions are traced in the scheme of Family 2.

FAMILY 3.

Family 3 is derived from Sting, who whelped a tan-headed and tan-marked bitch, Grove Nettle, in 1862, by Grove Tartar, a Hunt terrier.

The family has produced :—

Ch. Rachel, Ch. Sutton Veda (dam of Ch. Splinter, the founder of Line S), Ch. Olive (dam of Ch. Cracknell), Ch. Hester Sorrel, Ch. Glory Quayle, Ch. The Sylph, Ch. Ingatestone Royda, Ch. Cromwell Dark Girl, Ch. Southbro' Satchel, Ch. Misfit, Ch. Cromwell Miss Legacy, Ch. Dunsting, Ch. Chosen Damsel of Notts, Ch. Choicest Donna of Notts, and Ch. Mint.

Ch. Kinver, by Ch. Dandyford, born 1917.

And the dams of :—

Ch. Result, Ch. Adam Bede, Ch. Leander, Ch. Orkadian, Ch. Waterman, Ch. Monkshood, Ch. King's Shilling, Ch. Myrtus, Ch. Wrose Indelible, Ch. Cromwell Superb's Replica, and Ch. Semloh Superman.

Here, again, Grove Nettle's descendants have done so much in the past that it is quite possible that the former glories of this family may be revived. Only one bitch such as Dinah Morris would suffice, and her name may becomingly prove to be Modesty.

A picture painted in the early sixties by Mr. W. E. Turner contains a representation of Grove Nettle, who is the dam of Ruby, spoken of before, and the original founder of Family 3, born in 1862. She has a tan-marked head, with a partial blaze ; a sloping tan mark on her near shoulder (always a welcome gift of fortune !), and a tan mark at the root of and extending up the tail. She has a lovely deep short-coupled body, excellent ribs, and a long, well-placed neck ; good legs and capital feet, and that rare, strong, forceful muzzle and jaw which we shall even yet lose if we consent to the Borzoi type of long, thin, frail heads, which some modern judges are still favouring in the show ring.

Another picture, obviously by the same painter, represents some famous terriers. Among them is a very delightful portrait of Ruby, born in 1864, which would do real credit to Hedges or Reveley. This Ruby (b.) is a daughter of Grove Nettle, the founder of Family 3, and is the direct ancestress in tail female of Ch. Wrose Indelible and Ch. Cromwell Miss Legacy, in twenty-two generations, of Ch. Orkadian and Ch. Misfit in seventeen generations, of Ch. The Sylph in twelve, and of Ch. Olive and Ch. Splinter (founder of So line) in five and four generations respectively. Ruby appears to have been slightly spotted with black. The special interest in the picture, which was probably painted about the year 1871 (when the writer was too busy getting born to attend much to terrier-breeding), is that while it is easy to find fault with the remaining fifteen terriers, who exhibit some very long backs, some apple-shaped skulls, some crooked fronts, some bulgy full eyes, some badly roached backs, and most of them fail very much in substance and bone, Ruby alone is short-backed, well ribbed, with a beautiful sloping shoulder, long neck and head, small ears and eyes, excellent quarters, perfect feet, with deep pads and large round bone, combined with obvious freedom of action and balance of poise. Easily a winner in the " class " as drawn, and of these sixteen terriers she alone has *any* living issue, and very nearly *every* living smooth to-day traces back to her in some way, and most of them in dozens of different ways. Ruby's obvious superiority over her rivals, as drawn by this contemporary, is so pronounced that, on this photograph being shown to a little girl of twelve, she chose Ruby as the winner in about thirty seconds, though the terrier is neither prominently conspicuous nor ideally posed in the picture.

Twenty-seven champions appear in Family 3.

FAMILY 4.

Family 4 was founded about 1869 by White Fairy I, the dam of Nettle, which is a name of distressing complications, for over thirty bitches of some note were called by it. There is no doubt that Ch. Doncaster Dauphine is descended from White Fairy I, and that ensures the maternal descent of her granddaughter Odonta's strain. This remarkable bitch, who was known as Glimmer, is the dam of Ch. Oxalis, grand-dam of Miss Watteau and of Ch. Kinver, and great-grand-dam of Ch. Watteau Surprise and Ch. Watteau Wanton. She had that happy trick, I remember, of springing high from the ground, all legs at once, in rollicking and boisterous joy, a sort of guarantee of prolific well-being. Odonta's record alone, however, is enough to illustrate the merits of this family and its possibilities :—

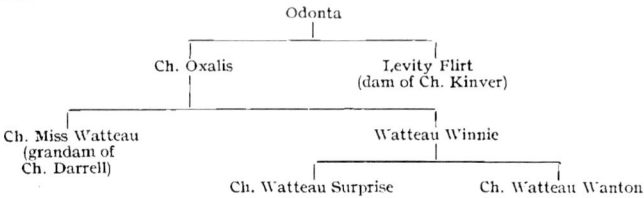

```
                        Odonta
                  |             |
           Ch. Oxalis        Levity Flirt
                          (dam of Ch. Kinver)
        |           |              |
Ch. Miss Watteau   Watteau Winnie
  (grandam of        |           |
  Ch. Darrell)  Ch. Watteau Surprise   Ch. Watteau Wanton
```

This family also produced Ch. Cromwell Tan Girl, a model terrier for a day's shoot, who knew the game from A to Z,

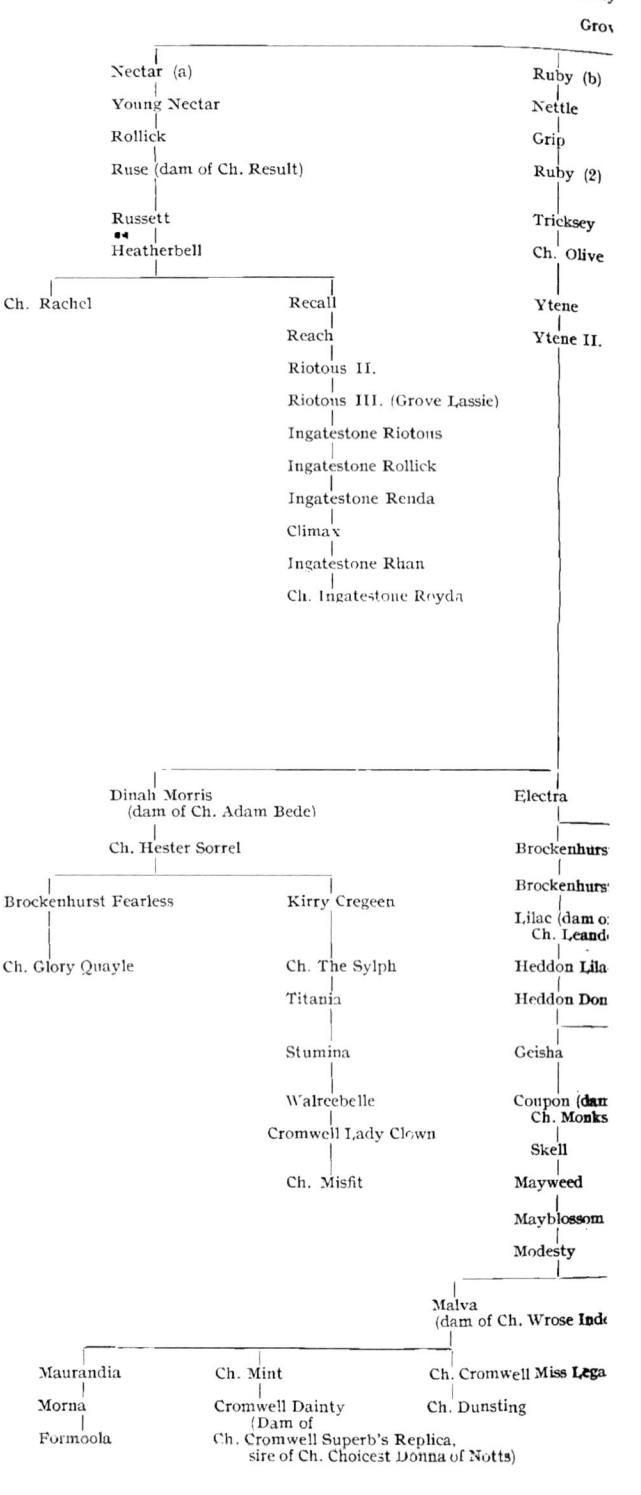

Rev. W. Handley
Grov
┌──┐
Nectar (a)   Ruby (b)
Young Nectar   Nettle
Rollick   Grip
Ruse (dam of Ch. Result)   Ruby (2)
Russett   Tricksey
Heatherbell   Ch. Olive
┌──────────────┬──────────────────┐
Ch. Rachel   Recall   Ytene
               Reach   Ytene II.
               Riotous II.
               Riotous III. (Grove Lassie)
               Ingatestone Riotous
               Ingatestone Rollick
               Ingatestone Renda
               Climax
               Ingatestone Rhan
               Ch. Ingatestone Royda

Dinah Morris   Electra
(dam of Ch. Adam Bede)
Ch. Hester Sorrel   Brockenhurs
┌────────────────────┬────────────────┐   Brockenhurs
Brockenhurst Fearless   Kirry Cregeen   Lilac (dam o:
                                                  Ch. Leand
Ch. Glory Quayle   Ch. The Sylph   Heddon Lila
                         Titania   Heddon Don
                         Stumina   Geisha
                         Walreebelle   Coupon (dam
                                                  Ch. Monks
                         Cromwell Lady Clown   Skell
                         Ch. Misfit   Mayweed
                                                Mayblossom
                                                Modesty

                         Malva
                         (dam of Ch. Wrose Inde
┌──────────────┬────────────────────┬──────────────────┐
Maurandia   Ch. Mint   Ch. Cromwell Miss Lega
Morna   Cromwell Dainty   Ch. Dunsting
Formoola   (Dam of
               Ch. Cromwell Superb's Replica,
               sire of Ch. Choicest Donna of Notts)

FAMILY 3.

```
's STING
    |
 e Nettle, b. 1862 (18 lbs.)
    |
    |_____
                    Tricksey (k)
                         |
                    Bitch by Trap
                         |
                       Giddy
                         |
                       Gaudy
                         |
        _____|_____
        |                                 |
      Freda                            Gradely
        |                                 |
      Freya                         Ch. Sutton Veda
        |                           (dam of Ch. Splinter,
  Saffron Charity                    founder of S line)
        |
  Brockenhurst Charity
        |
  First Favourite
        |
  Queen Rita
        |
  Rowton Veda
        |
  Elmhurst Veda
        |
  Elmhurst Venture
        |
       Nell
        |
  Rowton Peach
        |
      Dolly
        |
  Rowton Stellata
        |
  Cromwell Stella
  (dam of Cromwell Ochre's Legacy)
        |
  Cromwell Ochrette
        |
  _____|_____
  |                    |              |                      |
Ch. Cromwell Dark Girl  Boreham Ochrette  Ch. Chosen Damsel   Tan Lady
                         |                of Notts (dam of Ch.
                       Boreham Bertha     Chosen Don of Notts)
                         |
                       Boreham Bight    Ch. Choicest Donna
 Jessie              Pendant                  of Notts
 Violet        _____|_____
               |                |
            Diamond            Judy
               |                |
          Dark Diamond      Watcombe Tiny
               |                |
      Ch. SouthLoro' Satchel  Lady Babbie
                                |
           Princess Florizel  Lady Babbie II.
           (dam of Ch. King's   |
              Shilling)       Lady Claudia
                                |
 of                           Fay (dam of Ch. OrLadian)
 ood)
               _____|
               |                |
           Outshine         Little Fairy
               |             (dam of Ch. Waterman)
        Beechfield Outshine
               |
          Ch. Aire Belle

             |
         Martynia (dam of Ch. Myrtus)
 ble)        |
         Blink Blythley
             |
         Semloh Venturesome Lass
             |
         Semloh Bequest
         (dam of Ch. Semloh Superman)
```

Ch. Arrogant Albino, by Ch. Kinver, Jr.
Scottish, bred in 1921.

FAMILY 4.

WHITE FAIRY I, b. 1869
Arnold's Nettle (a)

- Needle (b)
  - Needy
  - Distaffina
  - Seamstress
  - Costume
    - Capucine
      - Carmen
      - Ermine
      - Prelude
        - Coleridge Peggy
        - Southlands Duchess
        - Ch. Cromwell Tan Girl (dam of Cromwell Raw Umber)
          - Stella
            - Jenny
            - Dot (by Wellesley Duke)
            - Tania
            - Pauline
              - Ch. Cromwell Dark Dorothy
                - Elvira
                - Elpatria
      - Cachuca
        - Camorra
        - Darkie
          - Ch. D'Orsay's Donna (dam of Dusky D'Orsay)
            - Cordova
            - Molly
            - Onda
            - Westville Enchantress
            - Vera Recina
            - Llandaff Dinah
              - Firenze
                - Dusky Dolly
                - Ch. Dusky Dinah
                - Flanchford Fay (dam of Ch. Cromwell Umber's Double)
      - Canttrip
      - Donttrip
      - Molly
      - Marinda
      - Melody
      - Margaret
      - Ch. Wrose Fanfare

- Nettle (2)
  - Verity (b)
    - Dahlia
    - Daffodilly (site of Pitcher, sire of Ch. Dominic)
      - Keetley's Daisy
      - Stainwith Bessie
      - Deyne Pearl
      - Harphurhey Lady Nell
      - Harphurhey Lady Oxon
      - Harphurhey Lady Mary
        - Harphurhey Pearl
        - Harphurhey Lucy
        - Ch. Heston Belle
          - Doncaster Dominetta
          - Doncaster Betty
          - Robin Repartee
    - Lilt
      - Outcast
      - Sunraine
      - Strife
      - Nell
        - Belmont Pearl
        - La Donna of Haydon
          - Ch. Doncaster Dauphine
          - Doncaster Ducena
          - Odonta
            - Ch. Oxalis
              - Kimlette
              - Kinlark Wendy
              - Tissot
              - Ch. Dunesgate Diana
                - Ch. Miss Watteau
                  - Watteau Winnie
                    - Ch. Watteau Surprise
                    - Ch. Watteau Wanton
  - Fly (b)
  - Viola (a)
    - Belgrave Viola
    - Dulcie
      - Lyons Salvella
        - Lyons Nettle
        - Ch. Lyons Sting
        - Dam of Queenie
          - Queenie
          - Stourbridge Fury
            - Stour Surprise
            - Blondinette
            - Swinford Superior
              - Ch. Swinford Sonia
                - Levity Flirt (dam of Ch. Kinver)
                  - Kidder Kit
                  - Quicksilver
                  - Lynhale's Resoub (dam of Ch. Charlton Aristocrat)
                    - Kidder Kinross
                    - Lady Mal
                    - Kidder Kountess
                    - Avon Ella
                      - Ch. Avon Snowflake (dam of Ch. Avon Stirling)
        - Dudley Gloom
        - Cornubian Ruby
          - Cyrene
            - Coronella
            - Chacona
              - Brook Barbara
              - Qui hi
                - Arden Jane
                - Arden Joan
                - Arden Gipsy
                  - Arden Sting (dam of Ch. Brockford Dandy)
                    - Arden Peeress
                    - Arden Patricia
                    - Sweet Dream
                    - Salt Town Queen
                    - Ch. Watteau Donzella
        - Quin
          - Rowton Rhona
          - Rowton Rosa
          - Rowton Peggy
  - Black eyed Susan
  - My Sweetheart
  - Sweet Olive
  - Sutton Viola
  - Souvain (reg. Mar., 1888)
  - Royal Sovereign
  - Battles Vinolia
  - Battles Merryweather (dam of Ch. Doncaster Dodger and Ch. Doncaster Dominic)

- Bergamot
- Shindy
- Bedford Brittle
- Ch. Blackrock Radiance
- Ch. Clytha Starlight (dam of Ch. Claud Duval)
- Clytha Comet
- Dudley Gambol (dam of Ch. Blizzard)
- Flowerdown

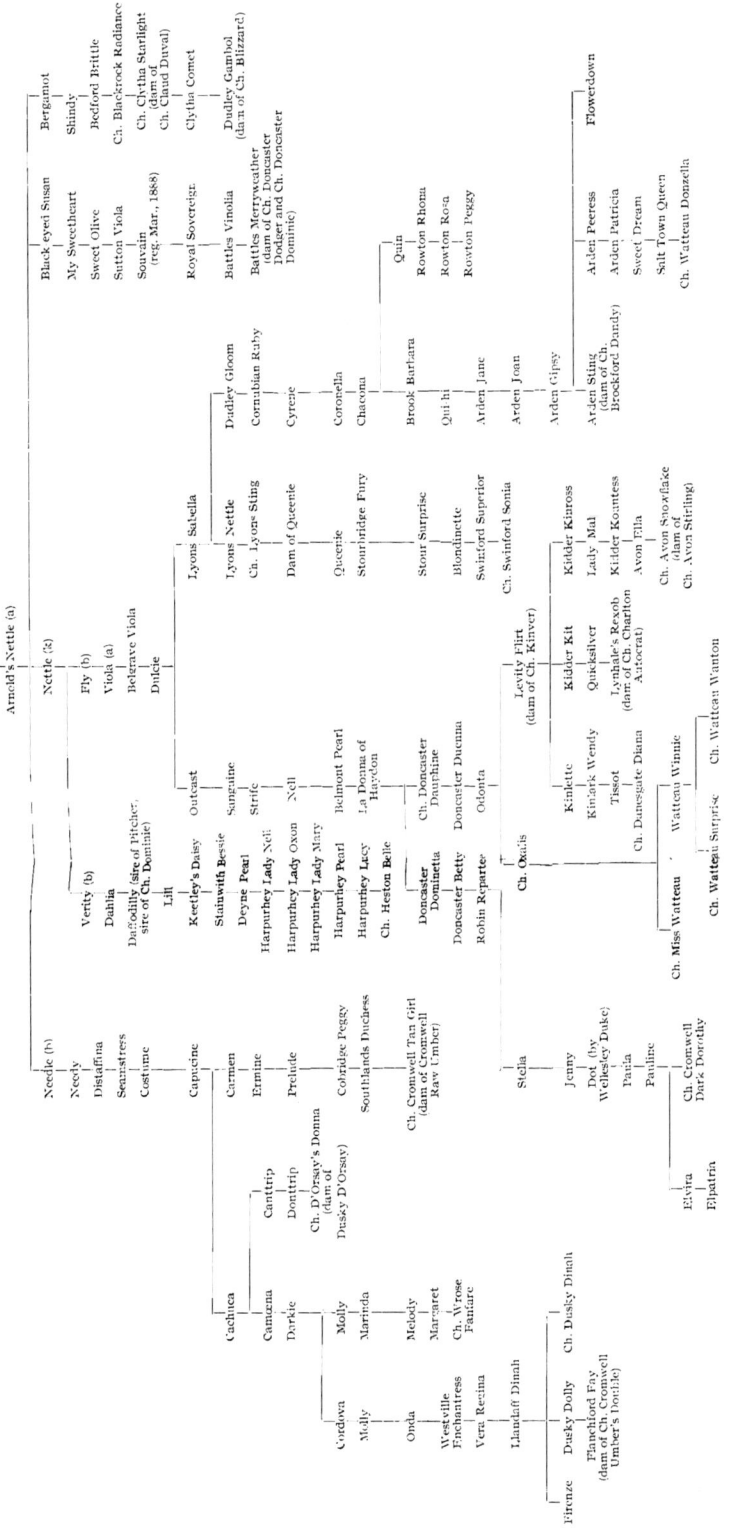

retrieving like a Banchory (as will most smooths who have half a chance), and the dam of Cromwell Raw Umber, the So dog, who sired a herd of champions, mostly bitches. Family 4 is also responsible for Ch. Dusky Dinah and for Ch. D'Orsay's Donna, the beautiful bitch deliberately selected to be the dam of the founder of the outcross line T, by an historic mating with a representative wire stallion. Twenty-seven champions are already recorded in Family 4.

FAMILIES 5 and 6.

Families 5 and 6 have produced but few outstanding terriers lately, and 7 to 22 have but one or two champions each.

It is worth notice that from these less successful families have sprung two of the best smooth dogs ever seen, in Ch. Levenside Luke and Ch. Raby Galliard, neither of whom did very much good at stud. Ch. Gypsy Joe and others still alive have a similar handicap in their stud chances by belonging to " one champion " families.

FAMILY 5.

```
Patch, 1876
 └─ Venom (d) (Tynedale Hunt)
     └─ Nellie (d)
         └─ Sample
             └─ Sunbeam (a)
                 └─ Sunflower
                     └─ Brockenhurst Fussy, b.1885
                         ├─ Barrowby Trixie
                         ├─ Barrowby Rene
                         ├─ Barrowby Sunbeam
                         ├─ Barrowby Sunshine
                         └─ Barrowby Pearl (B)
```

Barrowby Peerless
 └─ Rosebud (A)
     └─ Patch
         └─ Bedale Meg
             ├─ Lindon Marion
             │   └─ Morley Vixen
             ├─ Bebington Val
             │   └─ Bingham Snowgirl
             └─ Duchess Fortuna of Durham
                 └─ Bingham Floss
                     ├─ Lena
                     │   └─ Victoria Belle (dam of Ch. Neroford)
                     └─ Lady Leven
                         └─ That's Dunnit (dam of Ch. That's Rippin')

Ridgewood Selina
 └─ Elton Ringlet
     └─ Elton Una
         └─ Ch. Donna's Double

Ch. Lovaine (dam of Ch. Ridgewood Reckon) ─ Ch. Ridgewood Doris
Gyp (dam of Bramcote Carline)

Bramcote Charm
 └─ Flossie Clarke, 1903

Sabine Fantasy
 └─ Ch. Sabine Fad
     └─ Ch. Sabine Fernie
         └─ Ch. Sabine Forever

FAMILY 6.

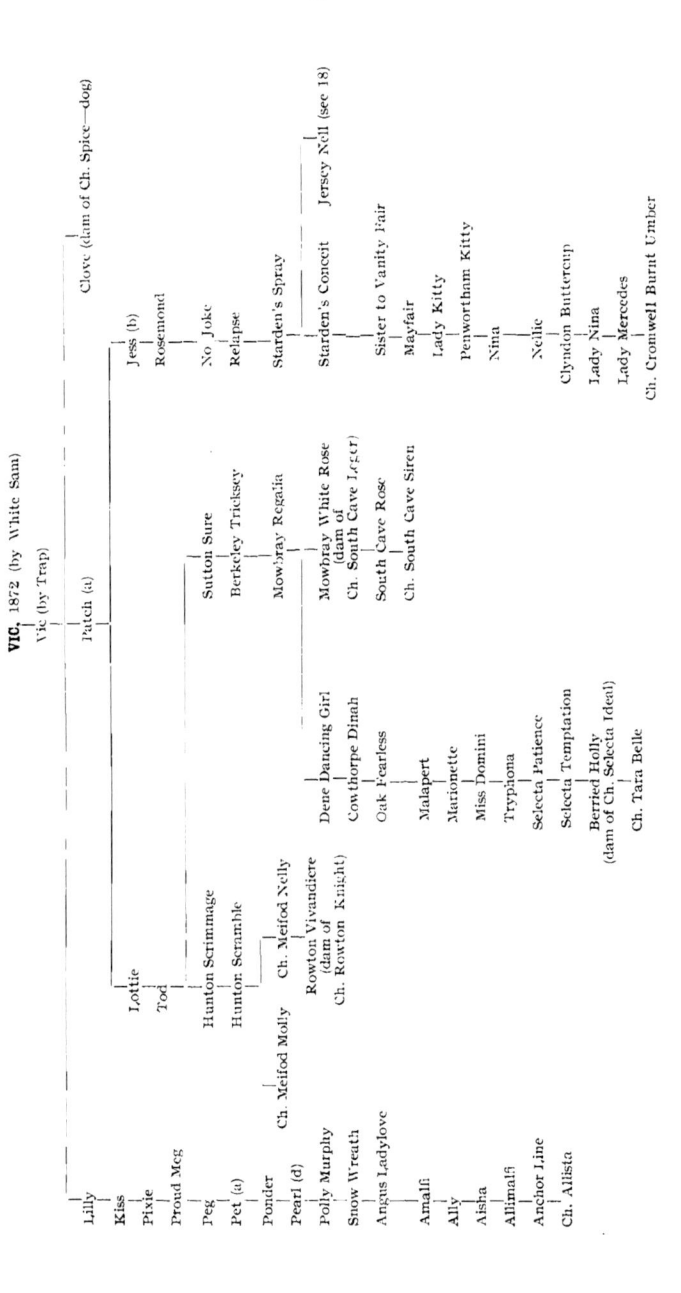

VIC, 1872 (by White Sam)
Vic (by Trap)

- Lilly
- Kiss
- Pixie
- Proud Meg
- Peg
- Pet (a)
- Ponder
- Pearl (d)
- Polly Murphy
- Snow Wreath
- Angus Ladylove
- Amalfi
- Ally
- Aisha
- Allimalfi
- Anchor Line
- Ch. Ailista

- Lottie
- Tod
- Hunton Scrimmage
- Hunton Scramble
- Ch. Meifod Molly
- Ch. Meifod Nelly
- Rowton Vivandiere (dam of Ch. Rowton Knight)

Patch (a)
- Sutton Sure
- Berkeley Tricksey
- Mowbray Regalia
- Mowbray White Rose (dam of Ch. South Cave Leger)
- South Cave Rose
- Ch. South Cave Siren

- Dene Dancing Girl
- Cowthorpe Dinah
- Oak Fearless
- Malapert
- Marionette
- Miss Domini
- Tryphona
- Selecta Patience
- Selecta Temptation
- Berried Holly (dam of Ch. Selecta Ideal)
- Ch. Tara Belle

Clove (dam of Ch. Spice—dog)
- Jess (b)
- Rosemond
- No Joke
- Relapse
- Starden's Spray
- Starden's Conceit
- Jersey Nell (see 18)
- Sister to Vanity Fair
- Mayfair
- Lady Kitty
- Penwortham Kitty
- Nina
- Nellie
- Clyndon Buttercup
- Lady Nina
- Lady Mercedes
- Ch. Cromwell Burnt Umber

FAMILY 7.

Many knowing breeders recognised that Ch. Levenside Luke would probably not, owing to his family extraction, sire a puppy nearly his equal ; yet they sent their bitches to him, not as a desperate hope (as their friends generally professed to believe), but on the sound principle that a dog of such outstanding points, though to some extent a " sport," must bequeath his points of progressive excellence to his ultimate progeny, and they were right in this. Though no outstanding good son or daughter was born to Luke, in spite of the fact that he had quite exceptional chances, still his influence has been by no means an ephemeral one. Here, for instance, are some of his male descendants, and their share of his extraordinary characteristics are probably more prepotently established in them than they were in him : Ch. Myrtus, Ch. Kinver, Ch. Arrogant Albino, Ch. Starling Surprise, Ch. Adonis, Ch. Avon Mainstay, and Ch. Wrose Indelible. But none of these are in tail male.

It will, however, be surprising news to many readers that Ch. Levenside Luke is the grandsire of more champions than almost any other stud dog in history ; and the fact that they are all out of his daughters, and not by his sons, will not escape the notice of the thoughtful breeder.

```
Gip
 |
Nell IV, 1879
 |
Madge (b)
 |
Matchgirl
 |
Daffy
 |
Avon Sooty
 |
Unnamed (Ch. Valuator) bitch
 |
Avon Vesta
 |
Avon Duchess
 |
Avon Daphne
 |
Levenside Duchess
 |
Levenside Lady
 |
Levenside Lisbeth (dam of Ch. Levenside Luke)
```

97

CH. DOMINIE, the original Jd.

DUSKY DIVER.

FAMILY 8.

As to the line and family of Jack the Diver, who had the honour of being the first challenge certificate winner after the war break, his line traces through Duke of Doncaster to Ch. Dominie, and back to Belgrave Joe, so he is Jd, and his family through Lady Sands, his dam, in twelve generations to a bitch called Rustic Queen, whom we all have been unable to trace further back. As she is the tail-female ancestress of Ch. Darrell, whose position bids fair to be lasting, and of Ch. Kitty Sparks, this is now an established family, and until some research reveals whence these bitches sprang, we have to call this Family 8.

As Rustic Queen obviously belongs to an earlier family, probably from the look of her progeny to one of the earliest, but so far no one has been able to reveal which, perhaps this note may be broadcast to someone who can help. If so, we earnestly beg him to reveal his secret. Meanwhile, Ch. Darrell and Jack the Diver are Jd 8.

Mr. Hargreave's Rustic Queen, 1884
  |
Hognaston Rose
  |
Dane Bessie
  |
Madeley Frantie
  |
Elmhurst Topsy
  |
Elmhurst Poppy
  |
Elmhurst Brownie
  |
Vanity
  |
Battles Mystery
  |
Christchurch Flo
  |
Christchurch Venus
  |
Lady Sands (dam of Jack the Diver)
  |
Ver Quiz
  |
Ch. Kitty Sparks
  |
Brinsop (dam of Ch. Darrell)

FAMILY 9.

Spot (by Rival), b. 1876
|
Effie Deans
|
Maggie
|
Belle
|
Needle
|
Belgrave Rose
|
Belgrave Dinah
|
Waveney
|
Dysart Fearless' sister
|
Minting Queen
|
┌─────────────┴─────────────┐
Grantham Queen   Minton Jess
| |
Barrowby Trifle   ┌─────┴──────────────────┐
| Richmond Grace   Leeming Lane
Barrowby Dame | (dam of Ch. Ridgewood Result)
| Raby Gertrude |
Barrowby Lena | Ridgewood Resister
| Lulsley Meg |
Drayton Bell | Ridgewood Rent
| Lulsley Lill   (dam of Ch. Ridgewood Re-echo)
Dark Vignette |
| Selecta Renown
White Slave |
| Ch. Selecta Discretion
Peggy
|
Kentish Kitty (dam of Ch. Kentish Despotic
and Ch. Kentish Despot)

101

Ch. Darrell, the war-time 1d sire.

Dusky D'Orsay, the first modern F. smooth
sire, by Dusky Collar (wire) ex Ch. D'Orsay's
Donna (smooth), born 1915.

FAMILY 10.

Grantham Nettle
Nettle (N)
Vivid
Pink
Proxy

Portia — Broseley Saucy
Countess Vigilantius — Broseley Raffle, 1888
Society Spy — Belvoir Duchess
(dam of Ch. Detector)
Belvoir Primrose
Winkie
Lady
Sunspots
Queenie
Broadgate Queen
Trinity Princess (dam of Ch. Cromwell Ochre)

Swingate Queen — Forrard

FAMILY 11.

Pink (of the Quorn)
Gipsy
Fussy (by Ragman)
Vexer

Banter — Vixen
Flora, K.C.S.B. 26551 — Fussy
Jessie — Winsome
Venus — Lady Welcome
South Cheshire Virtue — Blandford Spot
South Cheshire Sissie — Cowley Nellie
Dame Dalby — Cowley Pansy
Phœbe — Cowley Poppy
Phylloid — Cowley Pert
Cypher — Cowley Palm
Cappadocia — (dam of Ch. Kibworth Baron)
Ch. Cedilla (Ch. 1906) — (Ch. 1899)

FAMILY 12 (a branch of 2).

This family is clearly a branch of an earlier one, but, owing to the impossibility so far of tracing the unregistered Grace Newcombe, it is considered for the moment as a separate family. Mr. Tinne inclined to the opinion that Grace Newcombe was a mistake, perhaps for Ethel, but the records are emphatic as to her existence.

Apparently (Fox-terrier Facts in "*Our Dogs*," April 19th, 1929, and July 22nd and July 29th, 1927) Grace Newcombe is the daughter of Barrowby Prude, see Family 2, bred by Mr. Harry Newcombe, of Leicester and (as Mr. Tinne asserted) unconnected with his Newcomes with no *b*.

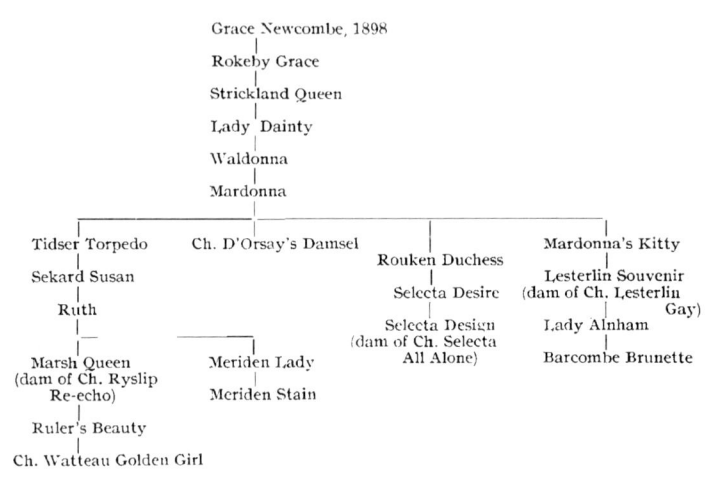

```
                    Grace Newcombe, 1898
                         |
                    Rokeby Grace
                         |
                    Strickland Queen
                         |
                    Lady Dainty
                         |
                    Waldonna
                         |
                    Mardonna
                         |
   ┌─────────────┬───────────────┬──────────────────┬────────────────┐
Tidser Torpedo   Ch. D'Orsay's Damsel          Mardonna's Kitty
   |                         Rouken Duchess              |
Sekard Susan                      |                 Lesterlin Souvenir
   |                         Selecta Desire       (dam of Ch. Lesterlin
Ruth                              |                              Gay)
   |                         Selecta Design         Lady Alnham
   |_____                |                      |
   |              |          (dam of Ch. Selecta   Barcombe Brunette
Marsh Queen    Meriden Lady     All Alone)
(dam of Ch. Ryslip  |
  Re-echo)     Meriden Stain
   |
Ruler's Beauty
   |
Ch. Watteau Golden Girl
```

FAMILY 13.

The six families, 13 to 18, are either extinct or in abeyance, but they have produced at least one champion each. So they are retained; their inclusion helps to illustrate very vividly the comparative hopelessness of breeding from stray excellence.

Old Vick (by Jock)
|
Young Vick (or Spot)
|
Beauty
|
Tiny
|
Squib
|
Rochdale Ruby
|
Kermincham Topsy
|
Kermincham Venus, b. 1884
|
Hatfield Nettle
|
Hatfield Pansy
|
Heroine
|
Bramcote Countess
|
Ch. Daintyford, b. 1912

FAMILY 14.

Branston's Vic, b. 1866 (White bitch whom Branston obtained from Peach, keeper to Lord Aveland)
|
Branston's Vic (by Twister)—(probably dam of White Fairy I, Fam. IV; see stud card of Tack)
|
(Given by Branston to Dr. Emms) White Vic, b. Jan. 30, 1888, dam of Old Belgrave Joe
|
Busy
|
Lady
|
Deacon Nettle, b. 1876
|
Deacon Rosy
|
Meersbrook Jeopardy
|
Peril
|
Dunstil Peril
|
Loughton Peril
|
Path Peril
|
Belmont Brigantine
|
Meifod Rachel
|
Meifod Ransom
|
Nada the Fair
|
Ch. Seven Trees Doris

FAMILY 15.

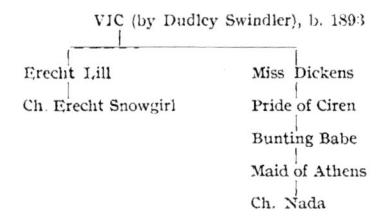

VIC (by Dudley Swindler), b. 1893
```
├─────────────────────────┬───────────────────┐
Erecht Lill                Miss Dickens
│                          │
Ch. Erecht Snowgirl        Pride of Ciren
                           │
                           Bunting Babe
                           │
                           Maid of Athens
                           │
                           Ch. Nada
```

FAMILY 16.

```
                                    Fussy
                                    │
                                    Lill
                                    │
                                    Pixie
                                    │
Fan                                 Fan
│                                   (K.C.S.B. 7000)
Burbie (by Tweezer), b. 1877
│
Busy
│
Hunton Skittles
│
Hunton Skitt, b. 1889
│
Hunton Ducibelle
│
Unnamed (sister of Vencer)
│
Spot
│
Chatter
│
Ch. Rant
│
Wicklow Sinfi
  (dam of Ch. Raby Galliard)
```

See K.C.S.B., vol. 24, p. 289, under Blackie; Burbie is by Tweezers II (Burbidge's, born 1875) ex Fan.

F.T.C.S.B., Vol. 1, has seven Fans, four too recent, three of unknown maternity! But Vol. 5 has a Fan (K.C.S.B. 7000) who may be Burbie's dam.

FAMILY 17.

Rose, b. 1882 (by Brockenhurst Joe)
|
Ness Myrtle, b. 1884
|
Ness Myrrh
|
Belmont Peach
|
Devona
|
Blight
|
Blaze
|
Bombardment
|
Sandown Baroness
|
Ch. Sandown Violet, b. 1903

FAMILY 18.

It was probably a mistake to call this a separate family ; it might have been *x* (unknown) ; but, once given, it would be a greater mistake to alter it. (*See* Family 6).

Jersy Nell
|
Vic
|
Sarnian Sceptre
(dam of Ch. Alport Derby, b. 1907)

FAMILY 19.

There is no evidence to identify this family with Family 2.

Arrowsmith's Nettle
|
Satire, b. 1870
|
Venom, b. 1873
|
Lotis
|
Sans Peur, b. 1875
|
Tidy
|
Fashion (b)
|
Beauty (j)
|
Dartmoor Cissie (Wire)
|
Carnage, b. 1886
|
Poulton Lottie
|
Poulton Pearl, b. 1890 (unreg.)
|
Humberstone Vice
|
Norton Tricksey
|
Norton Nellie
|
Brianette (dam of Ch. Gipsy Joe)

FAMILY 20.

Patrica (Wire)
|
Vic (cc), b. 1899 (Wire), by Ch. Meersbrook Ben
|
Linton Fury or Fairy
|
Pinper
|
Ch. Pinkie
|
Rustic Gipsy
|
Wharfeside Beauty
|
Ch. Myrtia of Ovington

FAMILY 21.

Cymbeline has become dam among others of Ch. Warbreck Spero (sire of Ch. Sulby Twink), and of Orkluke (sire of Ch. Starling Surprise and Ch. Adonis), and of Takeall. Cymbeline has proved a most remarkable and dominant factor, and it is the more unexpected in that her tail female is somewhat undistinguished from a classical point of view. Family 21 once looked as if quite soon that which was last might be among the first again. It remains to be seen if Cymbeline has produced a daughter as good in the nursery as her sons are in the ring.

Saltscar Masonda
|
Malice
|
Flowergirl
|
Proud Hope
|
Nanette
|
Cymbeline
(dam of Ch. Warbreck Spero and Orkluke, see Line S)

FAMILY 22.

As soon as the keepers of their own counsel reveal the identity of Love Lady's dam, this family will no doubt take its proper place under the wing of one of the great families, to which it very probably belongs.

Love Lady (unreg.)
Love Girl (unreg.)
Bandit's Princess, b. 1913
Declare's Model
Mymo (dam of Ch. Starling Surprise)
Lady Clare
Ch. Sulby Twink

FAMILY 23.

Vick, by Ragman
Violet, b. 1892
Hallgarth Vic, b. 1897
Hallgarth Vanta, b. 1907
Hallgarth Vantoi
Hallgarth Vhino
Arf and Arf
Ashbrook Alma (dam of Ch. Arrogant Albino)

FAMILY 24.

At last the family of Ch. Staunch Swell is established, and it has a special interest, for it links up two strains of bitches, one of the old times, and the other of great modern promise. To a beginner in our science will appear but a mere list of names; but to a student of the rock, from which modern terriers are quarried, it is full of suggestion and interest; for at the modern end it traces to Mr. Tose's Fly, from which many of Mr. Holgate's Southboro Surprises have had their origin, and to the late Mr. Jordison's successes about the time when his Marcon strain bid fair to monopolise the prize-lists; while at the other end we have the succession of good brood bitches, which Mr. Monson's Ebor prefix distinguish, leading to Cottesmore Tartaress, who was the dam of some of the late Mr. O'Connell's best terriers, beginning with Octave, which whelped Omen, the dam of Ominous, Ogre, etc., and the forbear of Oppidan, from whom sprang an army of great and good terriers ; it is very curious, however, that, as far as appears obvious at the moment, Ch. Staunch Swell happens to be the very first champion terrier which descends in direct maternal line from this rich bed of fruitful soil. The descendants of Patti therefore for the first time enter the list of champion-producing families, and as it would be obviously unfair to let so good a family be marked under the elusive x it is reasonable that we should recognise here a new Family with champion-producing potentiality, and it will be Family 24.

Patti (by Rattler)
|
Baby (b)
|
Bagley Bramble
|
Ebor Haste
|
Ebor Cinderella
|
Cottesmore Tartaress
|
Fair Flo
|
Madame Cronje
|
Bocking Peril
|
Bocking Prudence
|
Fide
|
Duchess
|
Marcon's Duchess
|
Gyp
|
Fly
|
Tournament
|
Cynella (dam of Ch. Staunch Swell)

INCOMPLETE.

Britton Madge
|
Britton Housemaid
(Reg. Mar., 1897)
|
Kirkmoor Bride
|
Mignon of Grays
|
Susannah of Grays
|
Western Belle
|
Scottow Supreme
|
Beau Queen
|
Aron Brunette
|
Kidder Kisabel
(dam of Ch. Little
Aristocrat)

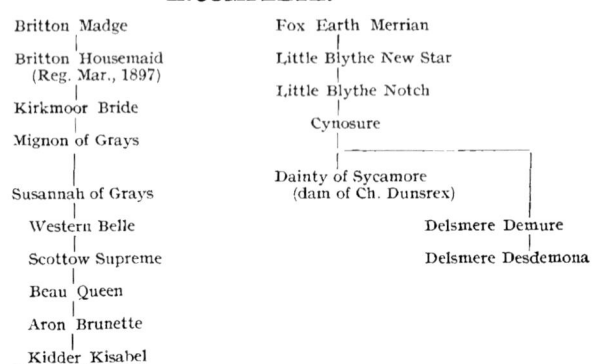

Fox Earth Merrian
|
Little Blythe New Star
|
Little Blythe Notch
|
Cynosure
|
Dainty of Sycamore
(dam of Ch. Dunsrex)

Delsmere Demure
|
Delsmere Desdemona

Successful Smooth Fox-terrier Breeders of the Century.

	Number of Champions Bred by each.
Mr F. REDMOND	9
Dr. MASTER	6
Mr. F. REEKS	6
Mrs. LOSCO BRADLEY	5
Sir JAMES HOSKER	5
Mr. F. C. BUTLER	4
Mr. J. C. TINNE	4
Mrs. BENNETT EDWARDS	4
Mr. J. G. A. JOWETT	3
Mr. J. W. HERRICK	3

CHAPTER VII.

SMOOTH FOX-TERRIER CHAMPIONS OF THE CENTURY.

DOGS.

Dog.	Sire.	Dam.	Birth.	Breeder.	Owner.
1901 Adam Bede, Jd 3	Donington	Dinah Morris	1896	J. C. Tinne	J. C. Tinne
Rowton Knight, Jd 6	Kibworth Baron	Rowton Vivandiere	1898	E. Powell	E. Powell
1902 Ridgewood Imperialist, Jd 2	Donatello	Barrowby Glisten	1899	T. A. Bradley	W. Musson
Ridgewood Result, S 9	Ridgewood Done	Leeming Lane	1901	A. Gillett	A. Gillett
Blizzard, S 4	Devastator	Dudley Gamble	1898	L. P. C. Astley	P. Howard
1903 Dukedom, Jr 2	Don Caesario	Duchess of Durham	1900	F. Redmond	F. Redmond
1904 Leander, S 3	Dauntless	Lilac	1901	J. C. Tinne	J. C. Tinne
South Cave Leger, S 6	St. Leger	Mowbray White Rose	1903	J. G. A. Jowett	W. Jordison
1905 Oxonian, So 2	Dark Blue	Overture	1902	D. O'Connell	F. Reeks
Ridgewood Reckon, S 5	Dark Blue	Lovaine	1903	A. Gillett	A. Gillett
1906 Doncaster Dominie, Jd 4	Duke of Doncaster	Battles Merryweather	1902	Mrs. B. Edwards	Mrs. B. Edwards
Doncaster Dodger, Jd 4	Duke of Doncaster	Battles Merryweather	1902	Mrs. B. Edwards	Mrs. B. Edwards

	Dog.	Sire.	Dam.	Birth.	Breeder.	Owner.
1907	Captain Double, Jr 1	D'Orsay's Double	Cherry B	1902	Mrs. J. H. Brown	R. Crawford
	Raby Galliard, Jr 16	Pendarren	Wicklow Sinfi	1903	W. I. Geff	Dr. Bruce
	Dete					nond
1909	Avon xendale, So 2	Oxonian	Desiree	1905	F. Reeks	F. R s
	King Shilling, Jr 3	Merchant Prince	Princess Florizel	1906	Mrs. J. W. Burn	Mrs. W. Burn
	Ridg ood Re-echo, S 9	Sinopi	Ridgewood Rent	1905	A. Gillett	A. G tt
1910	Defa , Jd 1	Doncaster Dodger	Burton Nellie	1908	Miss Powell	F. R mond
	Drus So 2	Avon Oxendale	Bellerophon	1907	H. Cook	F. R mond
	Gyps Joe, Jr 19	Viscount Dufferin	Brianette	1906	F. A. Bottomley	F. A. 3ottomley
	Monl ood, So 3	Oxonian	Coupon	1907	Dr. Master	Mrs. sco Bradley
	Tally lo, So 1	Oxonian	Tariff	1906	H. T. Crosthwaite	H. T. rosthwaite
	Alpo. Derby, J 18	Subduer	Sarnian Sceptre	1907	H. G. Carthew	S. G. ix
1911	Orkn . So 2	Oxonian	Domino Blanc	1909	D. O'Connell	D. O nnell
	Watt ian, So 3	Billy Willan	Little Fairy	1910	Castle and Vivian	Castl und Vivian
1912	Dunl h, So 2	Dunboyne	Dulcet	1910	F. Redmond	F. R mond
	Nero d, So 5	Keltford	Victoria Belle	1910	G. Nicholson	F. H Radford
1914	D'Or 's Model, Jd 2	Defacer	Dulcinea	1910	F. Redmond	F. R mond
	Orka un, So 3	Orkney	Fay	1911	F. Reeks	Mrs. sco Bradley
1915	Dang ; Jd 1	Defacer	Court Beauty	1910	Major Crawford	F. R mond
	Leve de Luke, Jr 7	Wellesley Duke	Levenside Lisbeth	1911	R. Williamson	Mack ion and Macbeth
1916	Crom ll Ochre, So 10	Orkadian	Trinity Princess	1915	Mrs. Losco Bradley	Mrs. sco Bradley
	Danc ord, Jr 2	Wattoford	Gedling Dolly	1913	G. T. Brumby	Dr. J nce

113

H

SMOOTH FOX-TERRIER CHAMPIONS OF THE CENTURY—*(contd.)*

DOGS.

	Dog.	Sire.	Dam.	Birth.	Breeder.	Owner.
1917	Darrell, Jd 8	Ordnance	Brinsop	1914	Dr. Edwards	Rev. A. J. Skinner
1920	Blybro Top Note, So 1	Cromwell Ochre's Legacy	Blybro Mischief	1919	J. W. Herrick	J. W. Herrick
	Watteau Woodcock, T 1	Beau Warboy	Dandy	1920	F. C. Butler	R. Chapman
	Starling Surprise, So 22	Orkluke	Mymo	1919	J. Meek	W. Hill
	Kinver, Jr 4	Dandyford	Levity Flirt	1917	G. Grimley	Dr. Bruce
1921	Netswell Rioter, Jd 2	Village Squire	Avon Radne	1919	F. Reeks	N. Dawson
	Myrtus, So 3	Cromwell Ochre's Legacy	Martynia	1919	Dr. Master	F. Redmond
	Blybro Beggarman, So 1	Cromwell Ochre's Legacy	Blybro Molly	1920	J. W. Herrick	J. W. Herrick
	Warbreck Spero, Jd 21	Ch. Darrell	Cymbeline	1920	J. Fairhurst	J. Fairhurst
1922	Wrose Incelible, So 3	Cromwell Ochre's Legacy	Malva	1921	Dr. Master	Dr. Bruce
	Adonis, So 2	Orkluke	Freehold Duchess	1921	M. P. Jackson	Howard and Hill
	Lesterlin Gay, T 12	Dusky D'Orsay	Lesterlin Souvenir	1920	Mrs. Mower	J. H. Lambert
	That's Rippin, So 5	Blybro Top Note	That's Dunnit	1921	T. H. Day	T. H. Day
	Kingsdown Prince, Jd 1	Kingsdown Joffre	Jesse	1921	I. Bartlett	A. E. Bishop
	Avon Mainstay, So 2	Legacy Lad	Avon Rosary	1920	F. Reeks	F. Reeks
	Vortigern, So 2	Cromwell Raw Umber	Heartbroken	1920	Dr. Hosker	Dr. Hosker
1923	Arrogant Albino, Jr 23	Kinver	Ashbrook Alma	1921	Miss Webster	Miss Webster
	Kentish Despotic, Jd 9	Darrell	Kentish Kitty	1922	Mrs. Thurston	Mrs. Thurston
	Gay Lally, T 2	Lesterlin Gay	Dandy Duchess	1922	Heslip and Robso	G. A. Cowper
	Brockford Dandy, So 4	Southboro Sandman	Arden Sting	1920	F. Elsey	Mrs. Losco Bradley

	Dog.	Sire.	Dam.	Birth.	Breeder.	Owner.
1924	Red Flag, Jd 2	Brynhir Revolution	Anemone	1923	Sidney Castle	Sidney Castle
	Serpent, Jr 2	St. Patrick	Last Chance	1922	Dr. Hosker	Dr. Hosker
	Dunstyle, So x	Ark D'Orsay	Almond's Nell	1922	Mrs. Burton	J. R. Hunt
1925	Little Aristocrat, So x	Kidder Karzan	Kidder Kisabel	1922	Grimley & Clay	A. E. Bishop
	Kentish Despot, Jd 9	Ch. Darrell	Kentish Kitty	1922	Mrs. Thurston	Mrs. Thurston
	Selecta Ideal, So 6	Ch. Little Aristocrat	Berried Holly	1924	Mrs. Breeze-Hall	A. E. Bishop
	Ryslip Re-echo, So 12	Ch. Wrose Indelible	Marsh Queen	1924	A. C. McMinn	R. B. Beverley
1926	Swanpool Domino, So 1	Ch. Little Aristocrat	Blybro Treasure	1924	W. H. Herrick	R. E. Creasey
1927	Paddock Premier, So 1	Ch. Little Aristocrat	Ring Duchess	1925	F. Jones	F. Jones
	Hermon Heir Apparent, So 2	Ch. Wrose Indelible	Ch. Hermon Bequest	1925	Miss Emery	Tansy
	Staunch Swell, So x	Staunch Lad	Cynella	1925	J. Hopwood	T. Hopwood
	Charlton Aristocrat, So 4	Ch. Little Aristocrat	Lynhales Rexob	1925	L. K. Collins	S. Castle
	Cromwell Superb's Replico, So 3	Cromwell Superb	Cromwell Dainty	1926	Mrs. T. I. Bradley	Mrs. T. I. Bradley
	Cromwell Umber's Double, So 4	Cromwell Last of Umber	Flanchford Fay	1925	T. H. Heron	Baron Van Der Hoop
	Aire Captain, Jr 4	Ch. Serpent	Aire Surprise	1926	J. H. Taylor	J. H. Taylor
					Miss M. Pearson	Miss Pearson
1928	Rikki Tikki Tavi, So wire	Selecta Dictator	Colleen Patricia	1926	T. J. Hargest	S. Castle
	Hillbro Dandy, Jd 2	Bombardier	Sweet Refrain	1927	A. E. Bishop	Dr. Rosslyn Bruce
	Selecta All Alone, So 12	Ch. Selecta Ideal	Selecta Design			
1929	Avon Sterling, So 4	Ch. Selecta Ideal	Ch. Avon Snowflake	1928	F. Reeks	F. Reeks
	Chosen Don of Notts, So 3	Cromwell Desmond	Ch. Chosen Damsel of Notts	1928	Duchess of Newcastle	Duchess of Newcastle
1930	Dunsmarvel, So	Llandaff Peter of Delsmere	Biddy of Llandaff	1927	Mrs. Williamson	J. R. Hunt
	Semloh Superman, So 3	Semloh Captain	Semloh Bequest	1928	W. A. Holmes	W. A. Holmes
	Farleton Flavian, So	Watteau Battleshaft	Ch. Watteau Nanette	1928	F. Calvert Butler	Mrs. Roy Richardson
	Delsmere Democrat, So	Ch. Little Aristocrat	Okey Pokey	1928	W. Attwood	R. B. Sheehan
	Bowden Rakish, So 2	Bowden Hamish	Bowden She's Charming	1928	Capt. H. T. Crosthwaite	Capt. H. T. Crosthwaite
	Dunsrex, So 1	Whiteholme Aristocrat	Dainty of Sycamore	1929	P. S. Watkins	J. R. Hunt

SMOOTH FOX-TERRIER CHAMPIONS OF THE CENTURY—(contd.)

BITCHES.

	Bitch.	Sire.	Dam.	Birth.	Breeder.	Owner.
1901	Erecht Snow Girl, J 15	Dusky Judge	Erecht Lil	1895	A. McDonald	A. McDonald
	Lovaine, S 5	S. Leger	Flossie Clarke	1899	A. Gillet	J. B. Dale
	Rant, Jr 16	Don Caesario	Chatter	1898	V. B. Johnstone	Mrs. Burns
1902	Donna Fortuna, Jd 1	Dominie	Dame Fortune	1896	F. Redmond	F. Redmond
1903	Duchess of Durham, Jd 2	Durham	Duchess of Doncaster	1899	F. Redmond	F. Redmond
	Glory Quayle, Jr 3	Don Caesario	Brockenhurst Fearless	1901	J. C. Tinne	J. C. Tinne
1904	Cymro Queen, Jr 2	Twenty-Four Carat	Pembro Jewel	1902	J. G. A. Jowett	J. Hay
	Ridgwood Doris, S 5	St. Leger	Flossie Clarke	1903	A. Gillett	J. B. Dale
1905	Haydon Dark Ruby, Jr 6	Dukedom	Dark Germ	1902	F. Redmond	Mrs. Bennett Edwards
	Sandown Violet, S 17	Brian Newcome	Sandown Baroness	1899	G. C. Drabble	G. C. Drabble
1906	Doncaster Dauphine, Jd 4	Duke of Doncaster	La Donna of Haydon	1901	Mrs. B. Edwards	Mrs. B. Edwards
	South Cave Siren, Jr 6	Drewton Lustre	South Cave Rose	1904	J. G. A. Jowett	J. G. A. Jowett
	Cedilla, S 11	Durbar	Cappodocia	1903	Miss Grey	G. Raper
1907	Avon Music, So 1	Oxonian	Victorious	1904	Miss Powell	F. Reeks
	Seven Trees Doris, S 14	Dark Blue	Nada the Fair	1905	W. Houghton	W. Houghton

Bitch.	Sire.	Dam.	Birth.	Breeder.	Owner.
1908 Nada, So 15	Camp Wellington	Maid of Athens	1905	J. W. Tilbury	F. W. Bright
Doralice, Jr 2	Ducal	Donovine	1904	F. Redmond	F. Redmond
The Sylph, So 3	Verderer	Kirry Cregeen	1903	J. C. Tinne	J. C. Tinne
1909 Oxalis, So 4	Oxonian	Odonta	1907	D. O'Connell	D. O'Connell
Rhodaford, So 1	Oxonian	Langton Justice	1907	J. C. Truss	F. H. Radford
Southboro Sachel, So 3	The President	Dark Diamond	1906	P. Masters	J. J. Holgate
1910 Hildaford, Jr 1	Bramcote Courtier	Rhodaford	1908	F. H. Radford	F. H. Radford
Tawdry, So 2	Tallyho	Youngster	1907	Burrell	H. T. Crosthwaite
1911 Miss Watteau, Jr 4	Camp Watteau	Oxalis	1909	F. C. Butler	F. C. Butler
1912 Ingatestone Royds, Jd 3	Raby Ruler	Ingatestone Rhan	1910	H. D. Wraith	H. D. Wraith
Pinkie, J 20	Camp Watteau	Pinper	1910	Hon. Mrs. Barclay	Hon. Mrs. Barclay
Sabine Forever, Jd 5	Sabine Reckoner	Sabine Ferrier	1910	T. H. Farwell	T. H. Farwell
1913 Donna's Double, Jd 5	Gipsy Joe	Elton Una	1909	Capt. Clay	H. T. Crosthwaite
Watteau Surprise, Jr 4	Oppidan	Watteau Winnie	1911	F. C. Butler	F. C. Butler
1914 Brynhir Bunty, So 1	Waterman	Bridget	1912	W. S. Glynn	W. S. Glynn
Daintyford, Jd 13	Watteau Wonder	Bramcote Countess	1912	F. H. Radford	F. H. Radford
1915 Kitty Sparks, So 8	Orkadian	Ver Quiz	1913	Dr. Edwards	F. W. Bright
Watteau Wanton, Jd 4	Camp Watteau	Watteau Winnie	1912	F. C. Butler	F. C. Butler
1916 D'Orsay's Damsel, Jd 12	D'Orsay's Model	Mardonna	1914	J. H. Peacock	J. H. Peacock
D'Orsay's Donna, Jd 4	D'Orsay's Model	Don't Trip	1912	F. Redmond	F. Redmond
Help-a-bit, So 2	Octavius	Herbalist	1915	Dr. Hosker	Dr. Hosker

SMOOTH FOX-TERRIER CHAMPIONS OF THE CENTURY—(contd.)

BITCHES.

	Bitch.	Sire.	Dam.	Birth.	Breeder.	Owner.
1917	Swinford Sonia, So 4	Martinet	Swinford Superior	1915	F. A. Godfrey	F. A. Godfrey
1920	Cromwell Tan Girl, So 4	Tan	Southlands Duchess	1916	H. A. Rockall	Mrs. Losco Bradley
	Havoc, So 2	Octavius	Herbalist	1916	Dr. Hosker	Dr. Hosker
	Misfit, So 3	Orkadian	Cromwell Lady Clown	1919	Mrs. Losco Bradley	R. Waller
	Selecta Discretion, Jd 9	Tees Real Grit	Selecta Renown	1919	A. E. Bishop	F. H. Thompson
1921	Cromwell Dark Dorothy, So 4	Cromwell Ochre's Legacy	Pauline	1919	E. Turner	Mrs. Losco Bradley
	Cromwell Dark Girl, So 3	Cromwell Raw Umber	Cromwell Ochrette	1920	Mrs. Losco Bradley	Mrs. Losco Bradley
	Cromwell Burnt Umber, So 6	Cromwell Raw Umber	Lady Mercedes	1920	R. Huskinson	A. E. Holt
1922	Cromwell Miss Legacy, So 3	Cromwell Ochre's Legacy	Malva	1921	Dr. Master	Maharajah Pithapuram
	Dusky Dinah, So 4	Myrtur	Llandaff Dinah	1921	Mrs. Williamson	Maharajah Pithapuram
	Sulby Twink, Jd 22	Warbreck Spero	Lady Clare	1921	J. Meek	F. C. Howson
	Dusky Doris, So 2	Myrtus	Darkleg	1921	F. Redmond	F. Redmond
	Heston Belle, So 4	Cromwell Raw Umber	Harpurhey Lucy	1920	Capt. Newell	Capt. Newell
	Jilted, So 2	Cromwell Raw Umber	Heartbroken	1920	Dr. Hosker	Dr. Hosker
	Wrose Fanfare, Jr 4	Dandypat	Margaret	1920	J. Bullard	R. E. Williams
	Aire Belle, So 3	Cromwell Omen	Beechfield Outshine	1920	W. H. Fitter	R. H. Taylor
	Myrtia of Ovington, So 20	Cromwell Raw Umber	Wharfside Beauty	1919	Mrs. Carins	Mrs. Carins
1923	Dunsting, So 3	Cromwell Ochre's Legacy	Malva	1921	Dr. Master	J. R. Hunt
	Mumtaz, So 1	Wrose Indelible	Active Lassie	1923	J. Townson	F. W. Bright
	Hermon Bequest, So 2	Cromwell Ochre's Legacy	Margery	1922	J. Gander	Miss Emery

	Bitch.	Sire.	Dam.	Birth.	Breeder.	Owner.
1924	Allista, So 6	Avon Myram	Anchor Line	1923	Miss Webster	Miss Webster
	Chosen Damsel of Notts, So 3	Cromwell Raw Umber	Cromwell Ochrette	1922	Mrs. Losco Bradley	Duchess of Newcastle
1925	Kentish Effendina, So 2	Malus	Sandgirl	1924	Miss Bourke	Mrs. Thurston
	Mint, So 3	Cromwell Ochre's Legacy	Malva	1920	Dr. Master	Mrs. Losco Bradley
	Netswell Radiance, So x	Kidder Karzan	Lovat Lady	1924	C. Mills	N. Dawson
	Viva, T 2	Gay Lally	Flagon	1924	Capt. Vernon	Capt. Vernon
	Watteau Golden Girl, So 12	Harpurhey Vector	Patch	1924	S. Bolsover	F. C. Butler
1926	Dunsdryad, So x	Llandaff Peter of Delsmere	Biddy of Llandaff	1925	Mrs. Williamson	J. Ellison
	Selecta Melody, So 1	Ch. Selecta Ideal	Selecta Decision	1925	Crook	A. E. Bishop
	Watteau Nanette, So	Ch. Brockford Dandy	Brownhill Duchess	1925	Kenyon & Woolstenhelme	Calvert Butler
	Tara Belle, So 6	Ch. Little Aristocrat	Berried Holly	1924	Mrs. Breeze Hall	
1927	Avon Snowflake, Jr 4	Avon Rossiter	Avon Ella	1925	F. Reeks	F. Reeks
	Watteau Donzella, So 4	Ch. Avon Mainstay	Salttown Queen	1926	Spilsbury	Calvert Butler
	Ingatestone Jade, Jd	Ch. Kentish Despotic	Ingatestone Jessa	1925	H. D. Wraith	H. D. Wraith
1928	Hermon Endowment, So 2	Ch. Little Aristocrat	Hermon Dowry	1926	Miss Emery	Miss Emery
	Hainworth Jess, So	Ch. Little Aristocrat	Ingatestone Jay	1927	Miss M. Driver	Miss M. Driver
	Sampler Maymorn, So 2	Fern's Ideal	Manor Duchess	1927	J. Hardman	A. Monk
	Choicest Donna of Notts, So 3	Ch. Cromwell Superb's Replica	Ch. Chosen Damsel of Notts	1927	Duchess of Newcastle	Duchess of Newcastle
1929	Delsmere Dainty, So	Llandaff Peter of Delsmere	Skysail	1925	Laffan	J. R. Hunt
	Raine Rarity, Jr 2	Avon Rossiter	Crafty Chorus Girl	1927	N. A. Loraine	N. A. Loraine
1930	Autumn Tint, So	Ch. Selecta Ideal	Yeoman Yolanda	1927	H. M. Thompson	Mrs. Marsden
	Endon Dainty, So	Ch. Brockford Dandy	Endon Nippy	1929	H. R. Brown, junr.	H. R. Brown, junr.
	Danesgate Diana, So 4	Caravan Qui Vive	Tissot	1929	A. G. Lipscomlc	Maharajah Pithapuram

CHAPTER VIII.

CHALLENGE CERTIFICATES.

1926

SHOW.	JUDGE.	DOG.		BITCH.	
National Terrier	Mr. Bray	Ch. Selecta Ideal	11	Ch. Watteau Golden Girl	7
Cruft's	Captain Vernon	Ch. Selecta Ideal	12	Ch. Dunsdryad	3
Middlesex Hospital	Dr. Colmer	Ch. Swanpool Domino	3	Ch. Dunsdryad	4
Bristol	Mr. Glynn	Ch. Red Flag	9	Selecta Melody	1
Manchester	Mr. Parker	Ch. Selecta Ideal	13	Ch. W. G. Girl	8
Leicester	Mr. Dawson	Charlton Autocrat	1	Ch. Dunsdryad	5
Kensington	Mr. Herrick	Ch. Selecta Ideal	14	Ch. Dunsdryad	6
Ayr	Mr. Oldershaw	Ch. Selecta Ideal	15	Ch. Dunsdryad	7
Joint Terrier	Mr. Wraith	Ch. Selecta Ideal	16	Selecta Melody	2
Cardiff	Mr. Reeks	Ch. Selecta Ideal	17	Ch. Dunsdryad	8
Liverpool	Mr. Hunt	Ch. Selecta Ideal	18	Ch. Selecta Melody	3
Bath	Dr. Hosker	Ch. Selecta Ideal	19	Ch. Selecta Melody	4
Taunton	Mr. Dunford	Ch. Selecta Ideal	20	Ch. Selecta Melody	5
Richmond	Mr. Curl	Ch. Selecta Ideal	21	Ch. Dunsdryad	9
Edinburgh	Mr. Mackinnon	Ch. Selecta Ideal	22	Ch. Dunsdryad	10
Darlington	Mr. Radford	Ch. Selecta Ideal	23	Tara Belle	1
Leeds	Mr. Wallwork	Ch. Selecta Ideal	24	Tara Belle	2
Worcester	Mr. Gething	Ch. Selecta Ideal	25	Watteau Nanette	1
Brighton	Dr. Hosker (2)	Charlton Autocrat	2	Ch. Tara Belle	3
Belfast	Mr. Reeks (2)	Staunch Swell	1	Ch. Tara Belle	4
Newcastle	Mr. Bishop	Ch. Selecta Ideal	26	Watteau Nanette	2
Kennel Club	Mr. Loraine	Ch. Selecta Ideal	27	Ch. W. G. Girl	9
Scottish Kennel Club	Mr. Dunford (2)	Ch. Selecta Ideal	28	Ch. W. G. Girl	10
Bradford	Mr. Herrick (2)	Ch. Selecta Ideal	29	Ch. Watteau Nanette	3
Fox-terrier Club	Mr. Thomas	Ch. Red Flag	10	Ch. W. G. Girl	11
Metropolitan and Essex	Mr. Cooper	Hermon Heir Apparent	1	Ch. W. G. Girl	12
Bristol	Dr. Hosker (3)	Aire Captain	1	Towyn Rose Marie	1
Birmingham	Mr. Bradley, M.F.H.	Ch. Selecta Ideal	30	Ch. Watteau Nanette	4

1927

SHOW.	JUDGE	DOG.		BITCH.	
National Terrier	Mr. Bishop	Paddock Premier	1	W. G. Girl	13
Cruft's	Mr. Glynn	Staunch Swell	2	Alleyn Harmony	1
Manchester	Mr. C. Butler	Hermon Heir Apparent	2	Avon Snowflake	1
Bristol	Mr. Everill	Paddock Premier	2	Delsmere Dainty	5
Kensington	Mr. Edwards	Paddock Premier	3	Ch. W. Nanette	1
Ayr	Mr. Wallwork	Hermon Heir Apparent	3	Ingatestone Jade	1
Joint Terrier	Baron van der Hoop	Cromwell S. Replica	1	Watteau Donzella	2
L.K.A.	Duchess of Newcastle	Cromwell U. Double	7	Avon Snowflake	2
Bath	Mr. Castle	Ch. Serpent	4	Watteau Donzella	3
Cardiff	Mr. Hunt	Ch. Paddock Premier	4	Avon Snowflake	3
Caledonian	Mr. Winder	Ch. Ryslip Re-echo	31	Watteau Donzella	4
F.T.C.	Mr. Dawson	Ch. Selecta Ideal	1	Ch. Avon Snowflake	4
Bournemouth	Dr. Hosker	Kentish Squire	2	Ch. Watteau Donzella	4
Windsor	Capt. Crosthwaite	Cromwell S. Replica	3	Ch. Avon Snowflake	5
Metropolitan and Essex	Mr. Holgate	Staunch Swell	32	Towyn R. Marie	2
Taunton	Miss Emery	Ch. Selecta Ideal	3	Ch. Avon Snowflake	6
Liverpool	Mr. Buckley	Charlton Autocrat	2	Ch. Watteau Donzella	5
Richmond	Mr. Bradley, M.F.H.	Dandinno	1	Hermon Endowment	1
Darlington	Mr. Wraith	Aire Captain	2	Dusky Lorna	1
Leeds	Mr. Edwards (2)	Cromwell U. Double	5	Aire Beauty	1
Worcester	Mr. Cowper	Ch. Paddock Premier	3	Delsmere Diadem	1
Bolton	Mr. Radford	Cromwell S. Replica	3	Ingatestone Jade	2
Brighton	Mr. Thomas	Cromwell U. Double	3	Charlton Consequence	6
Belfast	Mr. Wallwork	Aire Captain	1	Ch. Watteau Donzella	1
Newcastle	Mr. Bishop (2)	Sandown Shrike	6	Hermon Endowment	3
Sheffield	Mr. R. H. Taylor	Ch. Paddock Premier	1	Ingatestone Jade	7
K.C.	Mr. F. Reeks	Rikki Tikki Tavi	4	Ch. Watteau Donzella	8
S.K.C.	Mr. Gilzean	Ch. Aire Captain	33	Ch. Watteau Donzella	4
Bradford	Capt. Vernon	Ch. Selecta Ideal	4	Ch. Ingatestone Jade	9
Vet. Col.	Mr. Parker	Ch. Cromwell U. Double	11	Ch. Watteau Donzella	10
Bristol	Mr. Glynn (2)	Ch. Red Flag	7	Ch. Watteau Donzella	3
Birmingham	Mr. Loraine	Ch. Paddock Premier		Ch. Hermon Endowment	

CHALLENGE CERTIFICATES—(contd.)

1928

SHOW	JUDGE	DOG		BITCH	
National Terrier	Mr. C. Houlker	Red Flag	12	Hermon Endowment	4
Cruft's	Mr. C. Butler	Ringstone Rompaway	1	Autumn Tint	1
Bristol	Mr. A. E. Bishop	Rikki Tikki Tavi	2	Dusky Lorna	2
Manchester	Mr. H. D. Wraith	Rikki Tikki Tavi	3	Hainworth Jess	1
Kensington	Mr. J. R. Hunt	Hillbro Dandy	1	Hainworth Jess	2
Ayr	A. Mackinnon	Wrose Ruler	1	Ch. Hainworth Jess	3
Joint Terrier	Sir James Hosker	Hillboro Dandy	2	Selecta Surprise	1
Bath	Mr. L. Bradley, M.F.H.	Ch. Rikki Tikki Tavi	4	Choicest Donna of Notts	1
F.T.C.	Mr. N. Loraine	Hillboro Dandy	3	Ch. Avon Snowflake	7
Liverpool	Mr. G. A. Cowper	Ch. Hillboro Dandy	4	Sampler Maymorn	1
Bristol	Capt. Vernon	Ch. Hillboro Dandy	5	Ch. Selecta Melody	6
Windsor	Mr. N. Dawson	Selecta All Alone	1	Sampler Maymorn	2
Taunton	Mr. F. H. Radford	Bowden Hamish	1	Delsmere Dainty	2
Bournemouth	Mr. F. Reeks	Ch. Rikki Tikki Tavi	5	Raine Rarity	1
Richmond	Dr. Ireland	Ch. Hillboro Dandy	6	Choicest Donna of Notts	2
Leeds	Mr. G. Wallwork	Ch. Hillboro Dandy	7	Sampler Maymorn	3
Darlington	Mr. J. R. Hunt (2)	Ch. Hermon Heir Apparent	4	Ch. Watteau Nanette	6
Cardiff	Mr. S. Castle	Semloh Huntsman	1	Choicest Donna of Notts	3
Worcester	Mr. A. E. Bishop (2)	Ch. Hillboro Dandy	8	Ch. Hermon Endowment	5
Bolton	Mr. G. A. Gething	Selecta All Alone	2	Ch. Watteau Nanette	7
Brighton	Mr. L. Bradley, M.F.H. (2)	Selecta All Alone	3	Ch. Choicest Donna of Notts	4
Belfast	Mr. W. Oldershaw	Ch. Selecta Ideal	34	Selecta Surprise	2
Newcastle	Dr. Rosslyn Bruce	Dunsmarvel	1	Aire Trixie	1
Sheffield	Mr. H. D. Wraith (2)	Ch. Hillboro Dandy	9	Ch. Watteau Nanette	8
Scottish K.C.	Mr. N. Dawson (2)	H'nwood Beau Brummel	1	Ch. Watteau Nanette	9
Kennel Club	Capt. Swaffield	Ch. Selecta Ideal	35	Ch. Choicest Donna of Notts	5
Birmingham	Mr. Reeks (2)	Ch. Selecta Ideal	36	Ch. Choicest Donna of Notts	6

1929

SHOW		JUDGE	DOG		BITCH	
National Terrier	Jan.	Baron van der Hoop	Ch. Hillboro Dandy	10	Ch. Sampler Maymorn	4
Cruft's	Feb.	Capt. Phipps	Verno	1	Ch. Watteau Nanette	10
Bristol	March	Rev. A. J. Skinner	Don of Moortoft	1	Arragon Sylph	1
Manchester	March	Mr. Radford	Chosen Don of Notts	1	Ch. Watteau Nanette	11
Kensington	April	Mr. Bishop	Ch. Hillboro Dandy	11	Delsmere Dainty	3
Bath	April	Mr. Dunford	Ch. Hillboro Dandy	12	Ch. Delsmere Dainty	4
Ayr	April	Mr. Arthur Cooper	Sandport Brigand	1	Ch. Watteau Nanette	12
Joint	May	Mr. Curl	Ch. Hillboro Dandy	13	Ch. Choicest Donna of Notts	7
F.T.C.	May	Duchess of Newcastle	Ch. Hillboro Dandy	14	Ch. Sampler Maymorn	5
Windsor	June	Major Swaffield	Chosen Don of Notts	2	Ch. Choicest Donna of Notts	8
Bournemouth	June	Mr. Radford (2)	Avon Sterling	1	Ch. Choicest Donna of Notts	9
Taunton	July	Miss Emery	Avon Sterling	2	Ch. Sampler Maymorn	6
Richmond	July	Col. Bourne	Aovn Sterling	3	Ch. Sampler Maymorn	7
Cardiff	July	Dr. Ireland	Dunsmarvel	2	Ch. Watteau Nanette	13
Darlington	July	Mr. Gething	Ch. Chosen Don of Notts	3	Ch. Watteau Nanette	14
Worcester	Aug.	Mr. Dunford (2)	Ch. Hillboro Dandy	15	Aire Winnie	1
Leeds	Aug.	Mr. Wraith	Ch. Avon Sterling	4	Ch. Watteau Nanette	15
Brighton	Sept.	Mr. Dawson	Semloh Superman	1	Raine Rarity	2
Belfast	Sept.	Mrs. Hughes	Ch. Sampler Maymorn	2	Ch. Sampler Maymorn	8
Newcastle	Sept.	Capt. Vernon	Semloh Superman	2	Sampler Maymorn	9
Sheffield	Sept.	Mr. Radford (3)	Farleton Flavian	1	Ch. Watteau Nanette	16
S.K.C.	Oct.	Capt. Crosthwaite	Darien	1	Raine Rarity	3
K.C.	Oct.	Mr. Castle	Ch. Hillboro Dandy	16	Ch. Sampler Maymorn	10
Bristol	Dec.	Mr. Reeks	Ch. Chosen Don of Notts	4	Ch. Selecta Melody	7
Birmingham	Dec.	Mr. Dawson (2)	Bowden Rakish	2	Ch. Sampler Maymorn	11

CHALLENGE CERTIFICATES—(contd.)

1930

SHOW.	JUDGE.	DOG.		BITCH.	
National Terrier	Mr. Bradley, M.F.H.	Ch. Chosen Don of Notts	5	Autumn Tints	2
Cruft's	Mr. Bishop	Darien	2	Autumn Tints	3
Bristol	Miss Emery	Farleton Flavian	2	Endon Dainty	1
Manchester	Mr. Wraith	Delsmere Democrat	1	Ch. Watteau Nanette	17
Kensington	Mr. Ellison	Dunsmarvel	3	Delsmere Dainty	5
Bath	Mr. Reeks	Ch. Chosen Don of Notts	6	Danesgate Diana	1
Ayr	Mr. Hunt	Semloh Superman	3	Endon Dainty	2
Joint Terrier	Mr. Loraine	Ch. Avon Sterling	5	Danesgate Diana	2
L.K.A.	Mrs. Hughes	Farleton Flavian	3	Endon Dainty	3
F.T.C.	Mr. Radford	Ch. Farleton Flavian	4	Ch. Choicest Donna of Notts	10
Taunton	Major Swaffield	Delsmere Democrat	2	Ch. Danesgate Diana	3
Windsor	Mr. Curl	Homestead Aristocrat	1	Ch. Danesgate Diana	4
Bournemouth	Mr. Dunford	Delsmere Democrat	3	Ch. Danesgate Diana	5
Richmond	Mr. H. R. Brown	Ch. Delsmere Democrat	4	Ch. Danesgate Diana	6
Cardiff	Baron van der Hoop	Chosen Ochre of Notts	1	Clown Girl of Notts	1
Darlington	Mr. Calvert Butler	Ch. Semloh Superman	4	Ch. Endon Dainty	4
Worcester	Mr. R. H. Taylor	Ch. Bowden Rakish	3	Ch. Danesgate Diana	7
Brighton	Mr. Glynn	Dunsrex	1	Ch. Danesgate Diana	8
Belfast	Capt. Phipps	Dunsrex	2	Nosbor Real Spice	1
Newcastle	Mr. Thomas	Ch. Semloh Superman	5	Ch. Danesgate Diana	9
Sheffield	Mr. Wallwork	Ch. Dunsrex	3	Ringstone Ruffle	1
S.K.C.	Mr. Reeks (2)	Ch. Dunsrex	4	Drungewick Peggy	1
K.C.	Mr. Dawson	Kipyard Taffy	1	Ringstone Ruffle	2
Bristol	Mr. Radford (2)	Ch. Dunsrex	5	Ch. Choicest Donna of Notts	11
Birmingham	Duchess of Newcastle	Ch. Bowden Rakish	4	Delsmere Desdemona	1

The numbers after the names of judges denote repeated engagements; those after terriers indicate the number of Certificates won.

CHAPTER IX.

FOX-TERRIER POINTS.

ANIMAL GRACE AT ITS HEIGHT.

The modern show fox-terrier is, like a fox-hound, bred on exactly the same lines to-day as it was fifty, or indeed a hundred years ago, and it is not subject to the changing whims of fancy : the standard, which was drawn up in 1876, has hardly been varied at all, and where it has, only to make it more explicit.

The figure can be well studied and the parts learnt from the diagram of Kinver, on the front page ; from this model we can also observe the points. To judge of the merits of a fox-terrier, the eye should light first upon his shoulder, which should be " long and sloping," that is, the line shown by the shoulder bone should be more nearly parallel with the ground than upright, giving a long line from the front of his chest to his withers ; this point really comes first, because without a good shoulder well laid back, neither a terrier, a horse, nor a human being can possibly have an attractive and graceful figure.

FROM SHOULDER TO HEAD.

After finding a satisfactory shoulder, the critic glances first fore and then aft to satisfy himself that the forehand and hind-quarters are symmetrical, well-balanced and without any obvious defect. From this general survey he turns to a closer examination of the second great essential, a good head ; it has often been said that, with most judges, the head counts fifty per cent. ; perhaps it did once, but now our standard judges are far more expert and well know that a head, however good, without a sound general frame, is like a clock with a decorative dial and no works. To try to describe a good head is probably waste of time ; a sportsman must learn the ideal by experience, but some of the pictures in this volume should prove helpful.

The ears and eyes should both be small, and the latter dark, coal-black for preference, and the mouth should be "level," that is, the upper teeth should close just over all the lower ones, and all be clean and white. With this long, lean head there should be a long, but muscular neck; it has been said that a long neck ensures a good shoulder and is nine points of the whole, but this is perhaps a little over-stated. First, shoulder; secondly, head and neck; then thirdly, comes the body, or "barrel"; and here very much depends upon the rib formation, which after all is the chief feature of the skeleton: the fore ribs should be "well-sprung," that is, arched or hooped, rather than flat, and the hind ribs deep, so as to retain body power and preserve the terrier from appearing "cut-up" on the under-line, like a greyhound.

THEN BACK TO BODY.

In general effect the body should be short, as short as possible, so long as the shoulders lie right back, and there is freedom for the hind legs to act without any tucked or stunted effect. Shoulder, head, and ribs; and now "quarters," which mean the hind legs and their adjustment to the body and the stern, or tail. The merit of this part of a terrier is its practical usefulness; the effect should be strong and up-standing, though the thigh should be long, and the stifle, or joint between the hip and the hock must not be too straight, or the terrier's action will be stilted, and his appearance cramped. The action of the hind legs, as the terrier goes away from you, should be straight and balanced, without a suggestion of twisting or "platting," and neither sprawly nor narrow, but just natural and sturdy looking in effect.

FORE-LEGS AND FEET.

A docked stern should be straight, or nearly so, springing out from the end of the back ("at the corner," as someone has suggested) and carried as nearly perpendicular as may be. The pictures give a good idea of this. Shoulder, head, rib, and quarters, and then come front legs and feet; the front legs must be as straight as possible from every point of view, they should be round and strong and reasonably stout, the feet round and compact with deep solid pads and with no turn either in or out.

JACKET.

Then comes the coat, which may be coloured anyhow, so long as white predominates, and neither brindle, red, nor liver occurs ; it is essential that the coat should be hard and bright (for a soft-coated terrier is an abomination, and a dull-coated one a desolation), and it should also be straight, flat and smooth, points which many breeders, and alas, some judges, overlook, thus permitting a short-haired " wire " to masquerade as a " smooth " ; it should also be dense and abundant, providing a good covering underneath and inside his hind legs.

SYMMETRY.

Shoulder, head, ribs, quarters, forelegs, and coat being satisfactory, the last point is general symmetry, both in motion and at rest ; the present book contains a chapter on this one point, which is to be reproduced in five languages (like an advertisement of fruit salt !), but symmetry briefly means literally " measuring together," and it involves a delicate adjustment of the whole body ; symmetry is almost as much in the eye and taste of the beholder, as in the outline of the terrier, and that is partly why certain jolly good sportsmen should never choose their own hunters, nor judge other people's fox-terriers ! Sad, but true !

To conclude then, there are many glorious things in the world, and perhaps the most beautiful of all is the human form divine, seen at its best in the perfect grace of the newly-matured youth or maiden ; but close upon that ideal follows the lovely grace of animal life, and this may be seen perhaps just about at its best in a good weight-carrying hunter, an old English gamecock, and a well-balanced fox-terrier. So, at least, think some of us.

CHAPTER X.

NOTES BY THE WAY.
THE SPIRIT OF A TERRIER.

The first fox-terriers were used for bolting foxes when the standard was drawn up, and our present terriers are descended from these fox-finders. Now, the standard was drawn up in 1876. Let us see how the So line, which produces nine out of ten of our present-day winners, stood at that time. Its founder was Ch. Splinter; his sire, Dickon, was bred by Mr. Luke Turner in 1879, and was the son of Hognaston Dick by Hognaston Willie, who was a son of Foiler, who was born in 1871, so this is the period in which the standard was being, unconsciously perhaps, planned and prepared. Foiler's dam was Judy, " a capital good one for all sorts of vermin "; his sire was Grip, who weighed 17 lb.; Grip was by Grove Willie, who weighed 19 lb., out of Vixen, a " kennel terrier as good as could possibly be, and would face anything above or under ground." The old huntsman who kept these terriers wrote in 1879 : " I never knew Willie or Grip or Joe (Foiler) but they would screw themselves into any earth to follow a fox." Grove Willie was out of Grove Nettle, born 1862, a bitch who almost lived underground, a game varminty sort, and founder of Family 3, which still " nicks " so amazingly with the So line, which sprang from it ; she was a bitch of 18 lb. All these weights are in working condition ; then, as now, a terrier in show form weighs from 1 to 2 lb. more. Someone is sure to assert that these dogs were too heavy or too big for work, but we merely want to know the facts, and to the writer, at least, neither size nor weight is an essential criterion to the excellence of a terrier. There are good big ones and good little ones, just as there is work for big ones as well as for little ones, and just as different hunting countries provide different requirements. Gameness is the essential factor in the essence of a terrier, and gameness triumphs over all disabilities ; it takes the big ones where little ones, not game, are crowded out or stuck ; it takes little ones through a day or on a journey

"Good Work!"

"A Nursery Party!"

where big ones, not game, must have a lift, or collapse. No better spiritualist exists than a terrier; his spirit makes vapour or muscle of mere dog-flesh to suit any emergency; it triumphs over limitations of size, of age, of distance, and even at times of sex ! Wonderful thing, the heart of a good terrier !

FOX-TERRIER VARIETIES : THEIR NAMES.

" Wire-haired Terriers " were first called " Fox-terriers " by the Kennel Club in its stud book of 1882 ; previous to that there were the two separate breeds, fox-terriers and wire-haired terriers ; up to the year 1878, that is during the first 20 years of Stud Book record from 1859, the Kennel Club regarded fox-terriers as sporting, and wire-haired terriers as non-sporting ; the word " smooth-haired," as applied to a fox-terrier, was first issued by the Kennel Club in its Stud Book for 1883 ; and in 1884 it was altered to " smooth-coated," which prevailed till 1897, when (apparently without any special authority) the phrase was changed to " smooth," which has survived, for want of a better, till to-day.

Now, although it is true that the Kennel Club regarded " Rough-haired terriers " as distinct from Fox-terriers until 1882, and considered the former " non-sporting " until 1878, it should not be forgotten that five years before the earlier date, that is, in 1873, Manchester classified " Rough-coated Fox-terriers," and Nottingham " Fox-terriers, wire-haired." As the Nottingham fixture was five months later than Manchester it would appear that the term " Wire-haired Fox-terrier " was first applied at Nottingham. Between these two meetings the Kennel Club held its " National Dog Show " at the Crystal Palace, but there the fox-terriers were quite distinct from the other two breeds, " Broken-haired Terriers " and " Wire-haired Terriers," the latter being won by Mr. Saunderson's " Young Tip," a son of the founder of the T line.

THE MARQUESS OF HUNTLY AND FAMILY 2.

How thoroughly the late Sir John Thorold did his work in drawing up the first Fox-terrier Stud Book is proved over and over again by those who try to get beyond its records. For instance, in his account of the tap-root dams of Family 2, he merely states Tricksey to be out of Lord Huntly's Venom, of which there is " no further information," which is exactly true so far as pedigree goes, and it was with pedigrees that Sir John was concerned. It is, however, none the less interesting to us who are breeding dozens, even hundreds, of smooth fox-terriers from this wonderful Family, to have at this late date, no less than 67 years from her birth, first-hand information as to the nature and character of this famous little mother in Terrierdom. The breeder of her daughter, Tricksey, was the present Marquis of Huntly ; and in a letter dated June 4th, 1929, he says : " Your letters have helped me to recall my terriers, and I got Venom from Morgan, the huntsman of the Grove Hounds ; she was all white, and one of the best in her work I have ever known. She ran with the Grove Hounds for two seasons before I had her. Her daughter, Tricksey, had a brown patch on her side, and brown tips to both ears ; her sire Tartar was similarly marked. I do not think Morgan gave me the pedigree of Venom." So this is the rock out of which we are hewing, and we are not ashamed ! From her we have our great brood bitches, such as our Avon Maries, Scofton Bettys, Lamorby Gwyns, Betsy Borlases, Harmonys, Avon Roulettes, Flagons, Marsh Queens, Rouken Duchesses, and Lesterlin Souvenirs, in our time ; and from her sprang such great winners as Ch. Vesuvienne, Ch. Duchess of Durham, Ch. Doralice, Ch. Herbalist, Overture, and Ch. Cymru Queen in the old times.

Lord Huntly's letters have given us an insight into the past, for which many will be very grateful, and here's to all, who at his age have the grace and good memory to hand down similar sporting traditions to those who are " yet for to come."

THE VALUE OF "CHAMPIONS."

An experienced breeder suggests that it is quite possible to exaggerate the importance of champions as such. He holds that many of our best terriers do not become champions, while many champions are not what they should be ! Well, but then are "senior wranglers" *always* the best mathematicians. Bishops *always* the best preachers ? Judges the best lawyers ? Editors the best journalists ? Derby winners the best horses ? Waterloo Cup winners the best coursers ?

Perhaps not, but you must have some acknowledged standard and, as Goethe says, "The greatest tragedy of all is the conditioned striving for the unconditioned." There have been some 300 Smooth and Wire champions this century, and one would very confidently pit these terriers against any other 300 terriers of the period ; and we must leave it at that.

A SHREWD PURCHASE.

The wisdom of a purchase of a stallion terrier with a ready-made reputation is often questioned : the writer can bear testimony to one such purchaser, who procured 25 years ago, for £20, a six-year-old champion, which earned £98 in stud fees, and was sold two years later for £20 ; he subsequently bought another champion for £63, and he earned £255, and died young ; he then bought a puppy for 50s., which earned £122 in stud fees ; later he bought another smooth fox-terrier for £45, which brought in £196 in stud fees, and was sold, after winning £32 in prizes, for £21 ; subsequently, he bought a champion for £70, and this one realised £308 in stud fees, and died young ; then one of his own breeding earned £56 in stud fees and £76 in prizes, and was sold later on for £15 ; another, bought for £13, won £40 in prizes and £53 in stud fees, and yet another cost £5 and won £38 at shows, and was sold for £50 ; lastly, this same owner bought a champion for £300, and realised just over £1,000, without showing him more than two or three times. Enough has been said to prove that the shrewd purchase of a terrier with a reputation is no midsummer madness ! It remains to be said that the purchase of a young puppy with neither maturity nor reputation for four, five, or ten pounds is far less certain to prove a lucrative investment, nor is it calculated to bring the same interest as the arrival of a selection of good brood bitches from other kennels ensures, though, of course, it has other compensations. A cynic recently estimated that of the dog puppies sold for a "fiver" not a third reached maturity (but this is surely wrong !) ; of his third, he declared, not a fifth were show specimens, and of this fifth not a tenth became advertised stud dogs of reputation, so that to make sure of procuring such a real representative of the breed an investor would have to lay out 3 x 5 x 10 "fivers," or £750, whereas for a tenth part of that he could procure the ready-made goods : the moral was that from a financial viewpoint at least, a mature terrier with a reputation was a far wiser purchase than a "lucky-dip" shot at a puppy. But then it is so much more easy to find the small sum ; and perhaps that is just why the full-grown terrier is the better investment.

THE FOX-TERRIER CLUB SHOW JUDGES.

The list of those who have judged at the Fox-terrier Club Show in recent years is :—

	Smooths.	Wires.
1913	Sidney Castle	A. H. Clarke
1914	Walter S. Glynn	J. H. Wright
1915	Frank Reeks	George Raper
1916	Robt. Vicary	Walter S. Glynn
1921	F. H. Radford	F. Calvert Butler
1922 (Apr.)	H. D. Wraith	H. G. Sellors
1922 (Oct.)	Sidney Castle	Robt. Vicary
1925	Frank Reeks	J. H. Wright
1924	F. Calvert Butler	G. S. Thomas
1925	T. Losco Bradley	The Duchess of Newcastle
1926	G. S. Thomas	Holland Buckley
1927	Neville Dawson	J. H. Wright
1928	N. A. Loraine	Walter S. Glynn
1929	The Duchess of Newcastle	E. R. L. Hoskins
1930	F. H. Radford	Capt. Phipps

THE 50 GUINEA CHALLENGE CUPS.

In modern times the Fox-Terrier Club's two Cups, one for each coat, are competed for only once a year, and the winner is assumed to be the greatest fox-terrier of its coat for the year ; the honour is greatly coveted all over the world, but British breeders value it chiefly if they have bred the winner.

Only six terriers have won the Cup without becoming full champions ; the first is Brockenhurst Joe in 1881 ; secondly, Bramcote Crichton in 1898 ; thirdly, the Duchess of Newcastle's Kibworth Baron in 1899 ; next Mr. Reeks' Avon Minstrel in 1901 ; and lastly, Mr. Redmond's Dunwing, and

Mr. Hunt's Dunsfire in 1921 and 1922. The most successful winners of all the series are Ch. Donna Fortuna, who won it 11 times in a period of seven years, and Ch. Result, who won it 12 times spread over five years ; but the white Ch. Vesuvienne had seven successes over four years, and Ch. Dame Fortune six wins over three years ; old Ch. Spice had five wins over four years, while Ch. Richmond Jack, Ch. Duchess of Durham, and Ch. The Sylph each won it three times ; and Ch. Avon Oxendale and Ch. Donna's Double each won it twice consecutively. Only one terrier has won it more than once since the war, and he is Ch. Selecta Ideal, who won it in 1925 and in 1927.

A POLL FOR SMOOTH FOX-TERRIER JUDGES.

In 1929 a plebiscite was conducted by one of the weekly papers for the twelve most competent judges of smooth fox-terriers, and the first eleven chosen stood right away from the rest ; the voting was very spirited, and resulted as follows, the first twelve being now alphabetically arranged : Mr. A. E. Bishop, Mr. Losco Bradley, M.F.H., Dr. Rosslyn Bruce, Mr. Sidney Castle, Capt. Crosthwaite, Mr. Neville Dawson, Miss Emery, Mr. Walter S. Glynn, Mr. J. R. Hunt, the Duchess of Newcastle, Mr. Frank Reeks, Mr. Hildebrand Wilson. All these received over 200 votes, and all except one over 250 ; Mr. Calvert Butler had well over 150, while Messrs. Buckley, Holgate, Radford, Loraine, Parker and the Rev. A. J. Skinner, also scored well over a century, and some were close up to the 150 mark. Besides those who received over 100 votes, more than 50 votes were recorded for Messrs. Oldershaw, Nichols, Wallwork, Dunford, Wraith, Capt. Vernon and Dr. Master ; while a considerable number voted for Baron Van der Hoop, Mrs. Forsyth Forrest, Messrs. Thomas, Cowper, Curl, Gething, Mackinnon, Major Harding Cox, Capt. Wright, Capt. Phipps, Messrs. Warburton, Houlker, and Capt. Thurston, Capt. Denning, Capt. Swaffield, Messrs. Howard and Winder ; and among the tail appear about 40 other names who did not receive more than five votes each. That is, 20 judges received over 100 votes ; another 24 received considerable support. The astonishing thing is that nearly 300 lists of " most competent " judges arrived ; while it is pretty certain that, although many cards were anonymous, hardly any of the leading lights themselves—as, for instance, the members of the Fox-terrier Club Committee—sent in lists ; and it is quite clear that none of the " likely candidates " voted for themselves (or for anyone else !) The cards poured in from the North of Scotland to Devon, from Wales to Kent, and the postmarks indicate nearly every county in England, though London and Manchester predominate.

Mr. REDMOND ONCE ONLY "FAIRLY SUCCESSFUL" !

In 1881 the *Kennel Gazette* was started, and in its first articles on " Fashionable Kennels," chose as No. 1, " Mr. Redmond's Fox-terriers," and the author wrote : " There is nothing more difficult to breed than a first-class fox-terrier, and competition is rendered more keen from the fact that the breed is now excessively well understood, and the critics include some excellent judges of animal formation generally, and are almost super-critical over the points and perfections of a fox-terrier. Among those who have been fairly successful may be ranked Mr. F. Redmond, who commenced the formation of his kennel twelve years ago (that would be 1869 !), but it was some little time before he could get into the winning strain, as at first he bought his experience in the same way that others have done, by accepting too much what is seen at shows, without using judgment to discern the pure from the spurious. A total change was necessary, and a few judicious purchases furnished the material to ensure the probability of success. Legs and feet just like foxhounds should be pattern to follow, and on this point Mr. Redmond is crochety." " Crochety " is good ! We have good reason forty years later to be thankful for his crochets !

Mr. Redmond had a pretty large kennel, including Dugdale Joe, whose admirers regretted only the shade of his tan, which also slightly disfigured both the beautiful Ch. Olive of those days, and the far more beautiful champion, the best bitch of to-day. Tan should, of course, be of one shade throughout, and not clouded with brindly waves. But of greater interest to us was the " very pretty little dog with exceptionally good legs and feet," to wit, Dickon, the sire of

Ch. Splinter, and ancestor of all the Oxonian (or So) terriers alive to-day, which number some seven-eighths of all our winners. Among Mr. Redmond's bitches at that time was Ch. Diamond Dust, the tail-female ancestress alike of Dark Blue, of Ch. Oxonian, and of Ch. Adonis; her dam, Dusty, ran for four seasons with Lord Portsmouth's Hounds, and she herself was in the first class at work, and game to a fault.

Since then the number of big D's for which Mr. Redmond was responsible are innumerable; they came rolling down the years—D'Orsay, Despoiler, Dominie, Don Cæsario, Donnington, Dukedom, Defacer, and D'Orsay's Model; and, again, Dame Fortune, Donna Fortuna, Duchess of Durham, D'Orsay's Donna, and Dusky Dinah. Champions all, and more than champions. Some bought, but mostly home-bred, they formed a cloud of constellar glory which will never again be associated in such outstanding luxuriance with any single name; they blazed as an oriflamme on the shining forehead of the history of the breed, to entice us all on to the trail, not of hopeless emulation, but of grateful imitation.

THE DISPERSAL OF Mr. REDMOND'S TERRIERS.

On April 7th, 1927, at the Crystal Palace, Mr. Redmond's famous terriers were sold by auction for the benefit of the Fox-terrier Club. Nearly all the Committee and most of the members of the Fox-terrier Club were present, in recognition both of their respect for the late President and of his generosity in bequeathing his kennel to the Club. Besides them, many of Mr. Redmond's personal friends came, as did also a large number of others interested in so unusual a gathering. The bidding was limited to some twelve or fifteen people, and only eleven became purchasers.

The details of the sale are as follow:—

	Dogs:	Buyer.	Price.
1.	Deemster	Mr. Sidney Castle	£25
2.	Dusky Dominie	Mr. Neville Dawson	£42
3.	Dusky Dunlad	Mrs. Egerton Clarke	£57
4.	Drumhead	Mrs. Egerton Clarke	£8
5.	Dusky Dominie's son	Mr. J. C. Richardson	£5
6.	Dusky Dominie's son	Mr. J. C. Richardson	£5
7.	Dusky Ruler's son	Mr. Collins	£4

	Bitches:	Buyer.	Price.
8.	Dusky Dulcis	Mr. J. C. Richardson	£6
9.	Dusky Tansy	Mr. Sidney Castle	£37
10.	Double Fortune	Major Tudor Crosthwaite	£32
11.	Dusky Lorna	Mr. Sidney Castle	£50
12.	Dusky Margot	Col. Crawford	£23
13.	Deemster's daughter	Mr. H. A. Morris	£57
14.	Dusky Dominie's dghtr.	Major Crosthwaite	£40
15.	Dusky Dominie's dghtr.	Mr. B. F. Barker	£11
16.	Dusky Dominie's dghtr.	Capt. Fitzroy	£15
17.	Dusky Lorna's sister	Mr. Thrale	£10
18.	Dusky Ruler's daughter	Mr. Morris	£18

Mr. Castle's three purchases cost £112, Mr. Morris's two cost £75, Major Crosthwaite's two £72, Mrs. Egerton Clarke's two £65, Mr. Dawson's one successful bid cost £42, Col. Crawford's one £23, while Mr. Richardson's three acquisitions cost £16, Capt. Fitzroy's one £15, Mr. Barker's £11, Mr. Thrale's £10, and Mr. Collins' £4.

At the beginning of the sale a few onlookers, ignorant of the depth of sentiment that attached to this occasion, expressed surprise at the prices paid, but they soon realised that this was no mere mercenary estimate of commercial values, but also a tryst for the expression of practical devotion to an old friend and his favourites, every purchaser being fully alive to the exceptional nature of the gathering. For instance, there was no mistaking the attitude of Mr. Egerton Clarke, the industrious student of modern theories of breeding; his bidding on behalf of Mrs. Egerton Clarke made it abundantly clear that nothing in reason would prevent his purchase of that attractive little tan terrier, Dusky Dunlad, which shared with an unnamed bitch the honour of the highest price, for each realised £57.

The sale was an historical event, and it is improbable that we shall witness another such, though the example is a good one, and everyone present must have felt that no worthier, more generous, or more interesting plan for dispersing a valuable kennel could easily be devised.

MR. FRANCIS REDMOND, 1901.
Chairman of the Kennel Club Committee.

Mr. REDMOND'S ADVICE.

In 1913, just before the war began, Mr. F. Redmond wrote in a personal letter : " You will find a lot of pleasure in having even only one or two good smooth fox-terriers. I remember the time, years ago, when the claims of commerce engaged too much of my attention to have more than three or four bitches, what a lot of interest they gave me, and how I annually had a winner to run at our principal shows. I often think that the observant man who breeds only a few horses, a few terriers, a small head of poultry, or even cultivates a small garden of specialities, is frequently a sounder and more reliable authority than the great breeder, who is naturally more disposed to admit the element of chance to enter into his calculations." All of which is good, sound sense ; as well worthy of reproduction and remembrance to-day as when it was written.

RUBBISHY ADVICE !

As a contrast, it is almost unbelievable that there are still advisers to novices, who tell them that if a terrier is to be shown with a clean shoulder he must not be allowed to run about ! Was there ever greater balderdash? What? Has every foxhound and gundog living got bossy shoulders? Heaven help smooth fox-terriers if persons with these views get any sort of a hearing, for they would render the whole breed useless, stupid, and unsporting in a very few years. On the exact contrary, the less a terrier is shut up, the less likely is he to develop an ugly shoulder, and the only vestige of truth in the silly nonsense so often handed round is that, *if a dog must be shut up*, then he should be prevented from spending half his time and all his zeal in jumping up and down on his hind legs, a gesture which a free or well-worked terrier will very seldom adopt even for a moment.

Sir JAMES HOSKER'S PROMPTNESS.

An incident in the late Sir James' breeding operations, to which he often referred with amusement, occurred in 1916, when Ch. Dandyford was shown at the Fox-terrier Club Show in Nottingham, under the late Mr. Vicary. A " rough-and-tumble" took place between two over-game terriers in the ring, and as a result the thumb that holds this pen received a puncture, which still adorns it. The doctor, who was present, with his usual courtesy, produced from his pocket the necessary paraphernalia, and promptly cauterised the wound; finding it had been rather a bad one, a note of thanks was sent to the doctor, playfully suggesting the propriety of a professional fee. The doctor replied in similar mood that a service from the offending terrier would be more appropriate, and that he was sending an elderly matron to receive the perquisite; and so it came about that the veteran Pitapat, like Sarah of old, bore a litter of eight puppies to Ch. Dandyford in her old age. And here is the strange consequence, for if this litter had not been bred, the following terriers would not have adorned this planet : Ch. Vortigern, Ch. Serpent, Ch. Jilted, Ch. Gay Lally, Ch. Viva, Ch. Netswell Rioter, Ch. Red Flag, Ch. Hillboro Dandy, and many another good terrier which also descends directly from Pitapat's spirited little afterthought. Eight champions brought into the world at the price of a scarred thumb greatly amused the doctor.

" DOES TERRIER-BREEDING PAY ? "

As well ask " Does eating pay ? " " Does love pay ? " or " Does getting born pay ? " In breeding fox-terriers, at any rate, there is ample opportunity for anyone, with little or no capital, but with some spare time and an eye for an animal, to procure an absorbing hobby, with a reasonable prospect of considerable success, and the possibility of an outstanding triumph. The more a beginner relies at first on a trustworthy veteran, the sooner will he scale the bottom rungs of the ladder ; that once done, exercise of pluck in investment, training of the eye in judgment, application of brains, elbows and legs in preparation, skill and care in estimating character, human and canine, and a dozen other such activities, will be involved in answering the question whether it " pays " or no !

Whether it pays or not, fox-terrier breeding is a suitable hobby for a true sportsman.

What is a " sportsman " ? At a recent discussion at a Rotary meeting a definition of the term was invited, and finally a fox-terrier man's effort was accepted as holding the field. It ran : "A sportsman is one who finds his chief joy in the full use of all his powers in trying to make others use theirs, and who finds an almost equal delight in the success of either." Can any reader provide a better definition?

FERTILITY IN TERRIERS AND THOROUGHBREDS.

The *Bloodstock Breeders' Review* is full of suggestive matter for the scientific breeder. For instance, in a recent year 3,274 thoroughbred mares visited the 106 stallions which served more than 20 mares apiece ; of these only 2,012 had living foals, so that over one-third of the mares gave their owners no return for their year's keep and large stud fees. Those Early Victorian stick-in-the-muds, who refuse to recognise any new truth since they left school, and who concealed their ignorance by scoffing at all new hereditary knowledge, might learn at least a little humility by the study of the lines and families of thoroughbreds as dealt with in this *Review*. Fertility is shown to be a dominant feature of the Bend Or line of sires, for of the seven most fertile sires no fewer than six, all except the fifth, which is a Galopin, are of Bend Or's line. Of the 13 sires which stand at 400 guineas or more, no fewer than five are Bend Or's, and an attractive list they are—Colorado, Grand Parade, Manna, Phalaris, and Pommern ; and as with the " So " line in smooth fox-terriers, so with the Bend Or sires—their winnings in the year were easily more than those of any other two lines taken together. There is a curious parallel in these two dominant lines of horse and terrier progenitors, for if Oxonian is the equivalent of Bend Or, each had a famous progenitor, which begat other good lines still surviving. Oxonian had Splinter and Bend Or had Stockwell ; each again had in the remoter past an ancestor which had a world-wide reputation, Oxonian descending from the great Foiler, and Bend Or from Eclipse himself. While if we venture to compare the winning of the Derby with the winning of a championship, two very imposing lists can be drawn up of smooth fox-terrier sires in direct succession, thus Ch. Oxonian, Ch. Orkney, Ch. Orkadian, Ch. Cromwell Ochre, Cromwell Ochre's Legacy, Ch. Wrose Indelible and Ch. Hermon Heir Apparent ; or starting again at Cromwell Ochre's Legacy, Cromwell Raw Umber, Kidder Karzan, Ch. Little Aristocrat, Ch. Selecta Ideal, Ch. Avon Sterling, and Ch. Selecta All Alone. In the first line six out of seven successive generations of sires are champions, and in the second list seven out of ten are champions. These two lines represent the highest proportion of direct ancestors, which are champions, of any present-day fox-terrier stallions. Of Bend Or's direct line, the Derby winners include his sire Doncaster, his son Ormonde, and such subsequent winners as Flying Fox, Orby, Pommern, Grand Parade and Manna ; great horses and great terriers, but both great sires !

CROMWELL OCHRE'S LEGACY. So 3.

His record.

The greatest success of C. O. L. (as he was frequently called) sprang from alliances with Family 3 bitches, on the recognised theory of putting a sire to his dam's best blood. The real claim to eminent distinction, by which this famous dog will hand his curious name down to students of fox-terrier history in years not yet recognised in calendars, is difficult to epitomize. His four sons, which were champions, comprised Ch. Myrtus, Ch. Blybro Top Note, Ch. Blybro Beggarman, and Ch. Wrose Indelible ; and his five champion daughters were Ch. Cromwell Miss Legacy and Ch. Dunsting (these two are litter sisters of the last-named dog, and the litter is known to have changed hands at a sum of a little over £1,200), then came Ch. Mint of the same parents as those just mentioned, Ch. Cromwell Dark Dorothy, and Ch. Hermon Bequest, making nine champion terriers got by C. O. L. Of these, only one of the bitches, Ch. Hermon Bequest, whelped a British champion, Ch. Hermon Heir Apparent ; but of the four champion sons, Ch. Wrose Indelible sired three champions in Ch. Ryslip Re-echo, Ch. Hermon Heir Apparent, and the International Ch. Mumtaz ; Ch. Myrtus had two champion daughters in Ch. Dusky Dinah and Ch. Dusky Doris ; and Ch.

Blybro Top Note was the father of Ch. That's Ripping. So far, we have mentioned seven champion grandchildren, got or whelped by champions, but there are more to follow, for that good little sire, Cromwell Raw Umber, was also a son of C. O. L., and he is responsible for Ch. Vortigern, and the six bitches, Ch. Cromwell Dark Girl, Ch. Cromwell Burnt Umber, Ch. Myrtia of Ovington, Ch. Heston Belle, Ch. Chosen Damsel of Notts, and Ch. Jilted, doubling C. O. L.'s already mentioned grandchildren by the addition of another seven, to which must be added Ch. Avon Mainstay, a son of Legacy Lad, which makes the fifteenth champion grandchild. But even yet the tale is not completed, for Cromwell Raw Umber is the sire of Kidder Karzan, which has begotten a brace of champions, and the dog of this brace, Ch. Little Aristocrat, claims four champion sons and two champion daughters; and one of the former, Ch. Selecta Ideal, has sired two champion sons in Ch. Selecta All Alone and Ch. Avon Sterling, and a champion bitch, who share with Ch. Cromwell Superb's Replica (who is a son of Cromwell Superb, by Ch. Little Aristocrat) the honour of being champion great-great-grandchildren of C. O. L. Even yet there is more to add, for Cromwell Last of Umber, son of Cromwell Raw Umber, is the father of Ch. Cromwell Umber's Double; and Ch. Staunch Lad descends from Ch. Myrtus, while Ch. Allista is also of the royal (or "So") tail-male through Legacy Lad, and therefore the thirty-fifth British champion that has already been mentioned as tracing straight back in tail-male to Cromwell Ochre's Legacy. This is a record which will probably never again be equalled in the lifetime of any fox-terrier, and not his owner only, but the country as a whole, had very good reason to be superbly proud of him; although this review is limited to champions and their parents, other supremely good terriers have sprung from the same stock, and a search for a good smooth fox-terrier, "free from C. O. L. blood" is like looking for a humming-bird at the North Pole, or a fox in Leicester Square.

THE CHAMPION OF CHAMPION FOX-TERRIER SIRES.

There is no longer any question as to the fox-terrier who has proved the most successful of all time as a stallion terrier.

Capt. Phipps' wire, Talavera Simon, is the sire of :—

Dogs 7 (plus 2).	Bitches 7.
Ch. Bishop's Neglected.	Ch. Weltona Frizette of
*Ch. Talavera Gamester.	Wildoaks.
*Ch. Eden Aristocrat.	*Ch. Gains Great Surprise.
*Ch. Talavera Marcus.	*Ch. Newmarket Brandy Snap.
Ch. Weltona Pebble.	*Ch. Talavera Margaret.
Ch. Clonmel Ace of Ancon.	*Ch. Talavera Ethel.
Ch. Chantry Call Boy.	Ch. Kemphurst Creole.
and the	Ch. Petwick Cocktail.

American Champions—

Ch. (U.S.A.) Talavera Sunstar.
Ch. (U.S.A.) Simonson.

* International Champions.

That makes seven International champions, fourteen British and two American champions, consisting of nine dog champions and seven bitch champions; nor is it at all certain if the whole of the tale is yet told.

Here is an achievement which will indeed prove very difficult to surpass. It used to be thought that the performances of the sires, who thrived just after the war, when there were much fewer famous champions in competition, would never be equalled; but Simon has pulverised all their pride.

ELUSIVE GRACE NEWCOMBE.

About Grace Newcombe, the tail female ancestor of Ch. Lesterlin Gay, Ch. Ryslip Re-echo, and Ch. Watteau Golden Girl, many have not grasped the full difficulty. The late Mr. Tinne bred not only a litter, but numbers of terriers called something Newcome; and, as the affix was not reserved, others followed his lead, till there were literally hundreds of Newcomes, and a large number of Newcombes, chiefly got by Tom Newcome; but among these Grace Newcombe was inconspicuous—so much so, that both Mr. Tinne and his faithful old friend and henchman doubted her existence, and suspected that the famous Ethel Newcome was the dam of Grace Rokeby; this, however, has now been proved not to be so. Thanks to Mr. Hill-Wood, an old friend of the late

Mr. G. Raper, we now know that Grace Newcombe was bought by him from her breeder, Mr. Harry Newcombe, of Leicester, who was the owner of but three bitches : 1, Ethel Newcombe ; 2, Barrowby Prude ; and 3, Humberstone Girl (by Daddy ex Stirrup Cup's sister). Now, an inexperienced pedigree hunter would find enough circumstantial evidence here to assume that Grace Newcombe was the daughter of the well-known Ethel Newcome, because the former was bred by the apparent owner of the latter ; but no, Ethel Newcome was the late Mr. Tinne's famous little bitch born June 6th, 1890. She won at the Fox-terrier Club Show at Oxford, in 1892 ; and the judge, Mr. Pym, reported that but for her size (she only weighed 15 lb.), breeders should keep their eye on her and discard all other types. Well, she became, by Vis-a-Vis, the dam of the famous old Tom Newcome, sire of numerous winners ; *but* Ethel Newcombe had but one litter (3 dogs, 1 bitch) by Tom Newcome, and then died. So that, looking deeper, it is improbable that Mr. Tinne let his favourite Ethel Newcome go to Mr. Newcombe—and, even less probable, that the latter mated her to her own son ; it is far more probable that Ethel Newcome and Ethel Newcombe were distinct bitches, and more than possible that neither had anything to do with the elusive Grace Newcombe. Mr. Hill-Wood is very strongly of opinion that the lost dam of Grace Newcombe is Barrowby Prude (Bedale Dare Devil ex Barrowby Shining), and that the Newcombe affix is derived from the name of her breeder, and not from her dam. Mr. Hill-Wood bred Rokeby Grace from Grace Newcombe, and then sold her to Mr. Raper, who sent her to America ; it is possible that the American records of about 1900 may have in cold print the name of her dam ; if so, we should be glad to be assured that she is beyond any question the daughter of Barrowby Prude, which seems so highly probable.

SEX PROPORTION IN LITTERS.

Veda, who is a sister of the royal lady, Sandringham Lucy, produced lately six dogs and a bitch in one litter. Her gallant owner is very interested in the influence of special vitaminal diet upon sex, and had proclaimed his confidence that in this litter he could MAKE males prevail. Well, he certainly has !

His method is expressed thus: Nature would not permit an increase of females, which means the rapid increase of any species, unless there is a plentiful supply of food for that species; therefore we find well-nourished females tend to produce more females. On the other hand, where food is scarce (owing to conquest, over-population, or deliberate purpose) the predominance of progeny will be male. But as sex is determined during the early weeks of gestation, once a brood bitch is clearly in whelp generous nourishment will not affect the sex, but, on the other hand, will sustain the young males. Anyhow, Veda was very thin, and Veda had six males; to generalise with one, or even twenty cases, would be absurd, but this incident serves to illustrate a theory, on which systematic experiments are of interest. Geddes and Thompson's book is still about the best on predisposition to sex.

HEADS !

Technically, the head of a terrier is only worth 15 points in 100, but there are probably very few judges who think in these terms, and 50 per cent. is much more like the proportion which seems to prevail. The standard is certainly nearer what *should* be, but exhibitors are generally soon taught that the head must be almost beyond cavil, as any failing there is so very easily observed, and until public taste takes a turn, which it never has yet, the value of Family 3, with its "exaggerated" heads, will be a mighty asset.

TAILS !

Carriage of the tail has long been recognised as one of the most important features of that symmetry without which points, however good, avail but little. The tail must be put on at the right place—the corner !; carried at the right angle—the perpendicular !; and retained at attention—always ! But there is another consideration; the tail itself must be *convincing*. As in a horse, its substance is an index as to constitution at any rate, and probably as to character as well. To the unobservant, it is, as the late Hugh Dalziel said, "four contemptible little inches," but it must be remembered that it is only small because it is made so artificially, in order to distinguish it more easily from its quarry, and to relieve it of an easy point of attack. It is in reality the staff on which his flag was intended to fly ! It is the continuation of the vertebræ of the backbone, and also the handle by which a well-balanced terrier can be helped in all his good, and restrained from all his evil, works. A terrier's " starn " should be solid, sturdy and round ; it is his " handle," and denotes his rank, just as a title does that of any other nobleman !

SEE HOW THEY GROW !

This scheme for weights for puppies may be referred to as a permanent criterion. Health being normal throughout, it stands thus for an average dog puppy :—

Six weeks	3 lbs.
Eight weeks (after weaning) ...	3½ lbs.
Eleven weeks	6 lbs.
Fifteen weeks	8 lbs.
Twenty weeks	10 lbs.
Twenty-five weeks	12 lbs.
Thirty weeks	14 lbs.
Thirty-five weeks	16 lbs.
Forty weeks	17 lbs.

This might be hung up for puppies to study !

CRITICISM OF ALL-WHITE TERRIERS.

When a certain beautiful all-white terrier appeared some twenty-five years ago, her owner said, ' Watch for the first fellow who calls her head *Bull-terrier-like,* and I will show you the sort of ass who never will judge a fox-terrier.' " Bull-terrier-like " is the sheepish bleat that recurs with vacuous regularity whenever a white terrier is shown. Fox-terriers are *not* judged by their markings ! As well assert that a puppy, who drinks milk, is sure to have cat-like feet !

" NO BALL ! "

It was a delight to the ringside when Mr. Fred Mansell, who ought to know, told an exhibitor, who was showing under him, to " keep that silly ball still." The introduction of the pat-ball methods accepted in Toy breeds and a few breeds, chiefly kept as ladies' pets, is not to be encouraged among sporting terriers. Until a few years ago the thing was unknown, and it must drop back again as an unsporting experiment. An exhibitor lately asked a judge whether "balling his terrier for a week," would make him show better; and it was not till he had replied the dog did not appear to have worms as badly as all that, that he gathered that "balling" meant throwing a tennis ball to him to play with, as if the poor little sportsman was a dyspeptic kitten!

CONCLUSION.

Enough, perhaps more than enough, has been written to show the vast extent of our subject, and the far-spreading ramifications which arise from it. This volume is intended only to carry on the good tradition of our elders, and to bridge a gulf between them and those that are yet to come; the purpose is to provide material for the historian of the future, when our successors in the absorbing pastime of raising sporting terriers are anxious to look back to our day, for some measure of that guidance which we have gratefully inherited in what our fathers have declared unto us of the work of their days, and of the old time before them.

Index to Champions and their ancestors.

BITCHES.

	FAMILY
Absence	2
Active Lassie	1
Allista	6
Anemone	2
Arden Jane, Joan, Gipsy, Patricia, Peeress, Sting	4
Arf and Arf	23
Arnold's Nettle	4
Arrowsmith's Nettle	19
Ashbrook Alma	23
Atropa	2
Auburn	2
Avic Belle	2
Avon Bloom, May, Music, Myrtle	1
Marie, Marigold, Muffett, Radne, Rosary, Roulette	2
Snowflake, Ella	4
Daphne, Duchess, Sooty, Vesta	7
Baby	24
Bagley Bramble	24
Bandit's Princess	22
Banquet	6
Banter	11
Barcombe Brunette	12
Barley Beauty	1
Barmaid	6
Barrowby Deftly, Shifty, Shining Prude, Ramble	2
Pearl, Peerless, Rene, Sunbeamshine, Trixie	5
Dame, Lena, Trifle	9
Battles, Merryweather, Vinolia	4
Mystery	8
Beauty	2, 13, 19
Bebington Val	5
Bedale Meg	5
Bedford Brittle	4
Bedlamite	6
Beechfield Outshine	3
Belgrave Viola	4
Rose, Dinah	9
Belle	9
Bellerophon	4
Bellmaid	6
Belmont Pearl	2
Brigantine	14
Peach	17
Belvedere Model	2
Belvoir Duchess, Primrose	10
Bergamot	4

	FAMILY
Berkeley Tricksey	6
Betsy Borlase	2
Bideford Belle	2
Bingham Floss, Snowgirl	5
Bit 'em	2
Blackcap	2
Black-eyed Susan	4
Blackrock Radiance	4
Blandford Spot	11
Blaze	17
Blight	17
Blink Blythley	3
Blondinette	4
Blybro Mischief, Molly, Treasure	1
Bon Bouche	2
Borlase Shopgirl, Sultana	2
Bocking Peril, Prudence	24
Bombardment	17
Boreham Bertha, Ochrette and Bight	3
Bounty	3, 14
Bowden She's Charming	2
Bradley Victoria	2
Branston's Vic ('66), Vic (by Twister)	14
Bramcote Charm	5
Countess	13
Brianette	19
Briar Mintdrop	2
Brickdust	2
Bridget	1
Brinsop	8
Broadgate Queen	10
Brockenhurst Frolic, Vixen	1
Dainty, Dainty II, Dame, Gem, Lottery, Margaret, Waif	2
Charity, Fearless, Jessie, Tiny, Voilet	3
Fussy	5
Tiny	14
Brock-Worry	2
Brook Barbara	4
Broseley Saucy, Raffle	10
Brynhir Bantam, Buntie, Biss, Jennie, Bead	1
Bunting Babe	15
Burbie	16
Burton Nellie	1
Burton Wildbriar	3
Busy	14, 16
Busy (ex Damsel)	2

151

Index to Champions—(contd.)

Name	Family
Cachuca	4
Camœna	4
Camp White Woman, Winning Woman, Winnie, Water, Waterlily, Waxy	1
Cantrip	4
Cappadocia	11
Capucine	4
Carmen	4
Carnage	19
Cedilla	11
Charley's Aunt	1
Charlton Guinea Gold	2
Chatter	16
Cherry B.	1
Chimes	1
Choœna	4
Choicest Donna of Notts	3
Chosen Damsel of Notts	3
Christchurch Flo, Venus	8
Chuette	2
Climax	3
Clove	6
Clyndon Buttercup	6
Clytha Starlight, Comet	4
Cobridge Peggy	4
Cordova	4
Coronella	4
Cornubian Ruby	4
Costume	4
Cottesmore Tartaress	24
Coupon	3
Court Beauty	1
Cowley Nellie, Pansy, Poppy, Pert, Palm	11
Crafty Chorus Girl	2
Cromwell Lady Clown, Stella, Ochrette, Dark Girl	3
Tan Girl, Dark Dorothy	4
Burnt Umber	6
Crown Pansy	2
Cymbeline	21
Cymru Queen	2
Cynella	24
Cynisea	9
Cypher	11
Cyrene	4
Daffodilly	4
Daffy	7
Dahlia	4
Dainty	2
Daintyford	13
Daisy	2
Dane Bessie	8
Dame Dalby	11

Name	Family
Dame D'Orsay	
Dame Fortune	
Damsel	
Dandy	
Dandy Duchess	
Danesgate Diana	
Dareen	
Dark Diamond	
Dark Eyes	
Dark Gem	
Dark Pearl	
Dark Vignette	
Darkie	
Darkleg	
Darrell's Dame	
Dartmoor Cissie	
Daughter of Trap	
Daylesford Splinterbar	
Daze	
Deacon Diamond Nettle, Rosy, Ruth	
Death Struggle	
Deception	
Declare's Model	
Deftly	
Delecta	
Desiree	
Desiree's Lily	
Devon Gem	
Devona	
Deyne Pearl	
Diamond	2,
Diamond Dust	
Dinah Morris	
Directress	
Dirge	
Dirty	
Distaffina	
Dognes	
Doldrums	
Dolly	
Dominissa	
Domino Blanc	
Donation	
Doncaster Dominetta, Betty, Duenna, Dauphine	
Donna Dominic, Fortuna, Rosa, Vesta, Violette	
Donna's Double	
Donovine	
Donttrip	
Doralice	
D'Orsay's Damsel	
D'Orsay's Donna	
Dot	
Drayton Bell	
Dream	

Index to Champions—(contd.)

	FAMILY
Dryad	6
Duchess	24
Duchess of Doncaster	2
Duchess of Durham	2, 5
Duchess of Parma	1
Dudley Gambol	4
Dudley Gloom	4
Dulcet	2
Dulcie	2, 4
Dulcinea	2
Dundiver	2
Dunfly	2
Dunstable Princess	1
Dunstil Peril	14
Dura Darienne	2
Dusky	13
Dusky Bee	6
Dinah	4
Diva	1
Doris, Flo	2
Dust	2
Dusty	2
Dysart Fearless	9
Ebor Haste, Cinderella	24
Effie Deans	9
Eggesford Brick	2
Electra	3
Elmhurst Veda, Venture	3
Topsy, Poppy, Brownie	8
Elpatria	4
Elton Ringlet, Una	5
Elvira	4
Erecht Lill, Snowgirl	15
Ermine	4
Fair Flo	24
Fashion	19
Fay	3
Feather Weight	1
Feature	2
Fidget	2
Fido	24
First Favourite	3
Flagon	2
Flake	2
Flame	2
Flanchford Fay	4
Flodden	2
Floodgate	2
Flora	11
Floss	1, 2
Flossie Clarke	5
Flossie Velox	2
Flotilla	2

	FAMILY
Flowergirl	21
Fluid	2
Flutter	2
Fly	4, 24
Foresight	2
Forethought	2
Forrard	10
Frantic	1
Freda	3
Freehold Duchess	2
Freemanna	2
Frenzy	1
Freya	3
Frolic	1
Fussy	2, 11
Future	2
Gaudy	3
Gedling Dolly, Sceptre	2
Geisha	3
Giddy	3
Gipsy	11
Glorious	2
Glory Quayle	3
Good Enough	2
Grace Newcombe	2, 12
Gradely	3
Grantham Queen	9
Nettle	10
Grip	3
Grove Lassie, Nettle	3
Guinea Gold	2
Gyp	5, 14
Ha-ha	2
Hallgarth Vic, Vanta, Vantoi, Vhino	23
Halwill Vic	2
Hardpushed	2
Harpurhey Lady Nell, Lady Mary, Pearl, Lucy	4
Harmony	2
Hatfield Nettle, Pansy	13
Havoc	2
Haydon Dark Ruby	6
Heatherbell	3
Heddon Donna, Lilac	3
Helmet	2
Help-a-bit	2
Her Grace	2
Her Serene Highness	2
Herbalist	2
Hermon Bequest	2
Heroine	13
Hester Sorrel	3

Index to Champions—(contd.)

	FAMILY
Heston Belle	4
Hibernico	2
Highgate Bluebell	2
Hildaford	1
Hilltop Pearl	2
Hognaston Rose	8
Honey	2
Hospitality	2
Humberstone Vice	19
Hunting Day	2
Hunton Scrimmage, Scramble, Happy Eliza, Hesper, Bee I	6
Skittles, Skitt, Dulcibelle	16
Ickle Knut	2
Ingatestone Riotous, Rollick, Renda, Rhan, Royda	3
Jenny	4
Jersey Nell	18
Jess	6
Jessie	1, 11
Jill	1
Jingle II	1
Joyeuse	2
Juddy	1
Judith	1
Judy	3
Keatley's Daisy	4
Kentish Kitty	9
Effendina	2
Kermincham Topsy, Venus	13
Kidder Kit, Kinross, Kountess	4
Kinlark Wendy	4
Kinlette	4
Kinvara Blackie	2
Kirry Cregeen	3
Kitty Sparks	8
Koh-i-noor	2
La Donna of Haydon	4
Lady	10, 14
Lady Alnham, Dainty	12
Babbie, Babbie II, Claudia	3
Clare	22
Claudia	1
Kitty, Mercedes, Nina	6
Leven	5
Sands	8
Welcome	11
Langton Justice	1
Lappett II	2

	FAMILY
Last Chance	2
Laura II	2
Leah III	2
Leeming Lane	9
Lena	5
Lenore	2
Lesterlin Souvenir	12
Levenside Duchess, Lady, Lisbeth	7
Levity Flirt	4
Lilac	3
Lindon Marion	5
Linton Fury	20
Little Dorrit	14
Fairy	3
Llandaff Dinah	4
Lotis	19
Lottie	6
Loughton Peril	14
Love Girl, Lady	22
Lucky Dip	2
Lulsley Meg, Lill	9
Lydia Languish	2
Lyndhurst Vixen	1
Lynhale's Rexob	4
Lyons Sabella, Nettle, Sting	4
Madame Cronje	24
Madeley Frantic	8
Madge	7
Maid of Athens	15
Malton Nettle	2
Malva	3
Manor Duchess	2
Marceda	2
Marcon's' Duchess	24
Mardonna	12
Mardonna's Kitty	12
Margery	2
Marinda	4
Marsh Queen	12
Martynia	3
Matchgirl	7
Mayblossom	3
Mayfair	6
Mayfield Vic	1
Mayweed	3
Meersbrook Jeopardy, Madge, Modesty	14
Meifod Molly, Nelly Rachel, Ransom	6
	14
Melody	4
Meridan Lady, Stain	12
Merriment	1
Merry Sal	2
Minnehaha	2
Mint	3

Index to Champions—(contd.)

	FAMILY
inting Queen	9
inton Jess	9
isfit	3
iss Dickens	15
iss Milner	2
iss Watteau	4
odesty	3
olly	4
orley Vixen	5
oss I	1
oss II	1
owbray Replica, White Rose	6
rs. Fry	2
umtaz	1
y Sweetheart	4
ymo	22
yrtia of Ovington	20
h. Nada	15
ada the Fair	14
ancy Lee	3
anette	21
ectar	3
eedle	4, 9
eedy	4
ell	3, 4
ell IV	7
ellie	5, 6
ess Myrtle, Myrrh	17
etley	1
etswell Roulette	1
ettle	1, 3, 4, 10
ewton Vic	2
ina	6
o Joke	6
orton Trickery, Nellie	19
donta	4
kehurst Blue Stocking, Patience, Venom	2
ld Gold	2
ld Vick	13
live	3
nda	4
relle	2
ur Lilly	1
utcast	4
utshine	3
verture	2
xalis	4
aith Peril	14
aith Prim	1
atch	5, 6

	FAMILY
Patrica (Wire)	20
Patti	24
Paula	4
Pauline	4
Paviott's Blackie	2
Peg the Rake	2
Pembro Pearl, Jewel	2
Pendant	3
Penwortham Kitty	6
Perdita	3
Peri	3
Peril	14
Phœbe	11
Phylloid	11
Pink	10
Pink (Quorn)	11
Pinkie	20
Finper	20
Pit-a-Pat	2
Portia	10
Poulton Pearl, Lottie	19
Prelude	4
Preston Tiny	2
Pride of Ciren	15
Primrose Lass	2
Princess Florizel	3
Proud Hope	21
Proxy	10
Queen Rita	3
Queenie	4, 10
Quicksilver	4
Qui-hi	4
Quin	4
Raby Gertrude	9
Rachel	3
Rahatlakoum	3
Raine Rarity	2
Rant	16
Rarity	6
Reach	3
Recall	3
Relapse	6
Rhodaford	1
Richmond Grace	9
Ridgewood Selina, Doris	5
Resister, Rent	9
Ring Bridget, Duchess	1
Riotous II and III	3
Ripon Belle	6
Rivershy Duchess	2
Robin Repartee	4
Rochdale Ruby	13
Rokeby Grace	12

Index to Champions—(contd.)

	FAMILY
Rollick	3
Rosamond	6
Rose	17
Rosebud	5
Rowton Veda, Peach, Stellata,	3
Rosa, Peggy	4
Vivandiere	6
Royal Sovereign	4
Ruby I and II	3
Ruler's Beauty	12
Ruse	3
Rush	3
Russett	3
Rustic Gipsy	20
Queen	8
Ruth	12
Sabella	4
Sabine Fantasy, Fad, Fernie, Forever	5
Safety	4
Saffron Charity	3
Salt Town Queen	4
Sample	5
Sampler Maymorn	2
Sandgirl	2
Sandown Baroness, Violet	17
Sanguine	4
Sans Peur	19
Sarnian Sceptre	18
Satire	19
Scofton Betty	2
Seamstress	4
Selecta Desire, Design	12
Decision, Melody	1
Renown, Discretion	9
Semloh Venturesome Lass, Bequest	3
Sensation	4
Seven Trees Doris	14
Shindy	4
Skill	3
Sneyd Lady	2
Snowdrop	2
South Cave Rose, Siren	6
South Cheshire Virtue, Sissie	11
Southboro' Satchel	3
Southern Duchess	4
Souvain	4
Spot	13, 16
(by Rival)	9
Squib	13
Stamina	3
Star Turn	2
Stardens Spray, Conceit	6
Stella	4

	FAMILY
Sting	3
Sting Nettle I and II	1
Stour Surprise	4
Stourbridge Fury	4
Strangways Sublime, Sperance	2
Strickland Queen	12
Strife	4
Struck Out	2
Suffolk Rose	2
Sulby Twink	22
Sunbeam	5
Sunflower	5
Sunspots	10
Sutton Sure	6
Veda	3
Viola	4
Sweet Dream, Olive	4
Morsel, Refrain	2
Swinford Superior, Sonia	4
Swingate Queen	10
Sylph, The	3
Take Care	1
Tara Belle	6
Tariff	1
Tarolinta	1
Tell Tale	6
Terra	1
Terrible Calamity	1
That's Dunnit	5
The Sylph	3
Tidy	19
Tiny	13
Tissot	4
Titania	3
Tod	6
Tournament	24
Tricksey	2, 3
Trinity Princess	10
Twiddly Bit	1
Twiggle	1
Typist	2
Valetta	2
Valkyrie	2
Valley	2
Valse	2
Valuation	2
Value	2
Vanity	8
Varema	2
Vashti II	1
Vee	2
Vehement	2
Velzie	2

Index to Champions—(contd.)

	FAMILY
Vene (dam of Dominie)	6
Veneer	16
Venetia	2
Venom	2, 5, 19
Venus	11
Ver Quiz	8
Vera Regina	4
Verona	2
Vesuvienne	2
Vexer	11
Via	2
Vic	6, 15, 18, 20
Vick (by Ragman)	23
Victoria Belle	5
Victorious	1
Viko	2
Village Belle	2
Viola	4
Violet	23
Viva	2
Vivid	10
Vixen	11
Volatile	2

	FAMILY
Waif	2
Waldonna	12
Walreebelle	3
Walton Belle	5
Watcombe Tiny	3
Watteau Lily, Vixen, Water Ouzel	1
Winnie, Surprise, Wanton, Donzella	4
Golden Girl	12
Waveney	9
Westville Enchantress	4
Whattah Brownie	2
White Fairy I	4
White Slave Peggy	9
White Vic	14
Wickie	10
Wicklow Sinfi	16
Winsome	11
Wrose Fanfare	4
Yeovil Countess, Princess	2
Young Nectar	3
Vick	13
Ytene and Ytene II	3

DOGS.

	FAMILY
Adonis	So
Aire Captain	Jr
Ambrose Joe	Jr
Arrogant Albino	Jr
Avon Oxendale, Mainstay, Sterling Rossiter	So Jr
Beau Warboy	T
Bedale Dare Devil	S
Belgrave Joe	J
Belmont Ranger	S
Belvoir Joe	J
Billy Willan	So
Blybro Top Note, Beggarman	So
Bowden Rakish	So
Brock Joe, Jim, Rally	J
Brockenhurst Minor	Jr
Brockford Dandy	So
Bramcote Carbine	Jd
Camp Watteau	Jr
Capt. Double	Jr
Charlton Autocrat	So
Chosen Don of Notts	So

	FAMILY
Cromwell Omen, Ochre, Ochre's Legacy, Raw Umber, Superb's Replica, Umber's Double	So
Daddy	Jr
Dandyford	Jr
Dandypat	Jr
Dark Blue	S
Darrell	Jd
Defacer	Jd
Delarey	Jr
Despoiler	S
Dickon	S
Diving Jack	Jd
Dominie	Jd
Doncaster Dodger	Jd
Don Cesario	Jr
D'Orsay	J
D'Orsay's Double	Jr
Model	Jd
Dreadnought	S
Dufferin	J
Duke of Doncaster	Jd
Dunsany	Jd
Dunsmarvel	So

Index to Champions—(contd.)

	FAMILY		FAMILY
Dunsrex	So	Orkluke	So
Dunstyle	So	Orkney	So
Dunwing	T	Oxonian	So
Durham	Jd		
Dusky Diver	Jd	Paddock Premier	So
Dusky D'Orsay	T	Pendarren	Jr
		Pitcher	J
Eton Blue	S		
		Raby Galliard	Jr
		Reckon	J
Farleton Flavian	So	Reckoner	J
Flambro	So	Red Flag	Jd
Foiler	S	Regent	J
		Result	Jr
		Ridgewood Re-echo, Reckon	S
Gay Lally	T	Rikki Tikki Tavi	So
Gipsy Joe	J	Roysterer	J
Grip	S	Ryslip Re-echo	So
Grove Willie, Tartar	S		
		St. Leger	S
Hermon Heir Apparent	So	St. Patrick	Jr
Hillboro' Dandy	Jd	Selecta All Alone, Ideal	So
Hognaston Dick, Willie	S	Semloh Superman	So
Hunton Billy, Bridgeroom	Jr	Serpent	Jr
Tartar	S	Sinopi	S
		South Cave Leger	S
		Southboro' Sandman	So
Jack The Diver	Jd	Spice	J
		Splinter	S
		Starling Surprise	So
Kentish Despot, Despotic	Jd	Staunch Swell	So
Kibworth Baron	Jd	Stipendiary	J
Kingsdown General, Prince	Jd	Swanpool Domino	So
Kinver	Jr		
		Tally Ho	S
Legacy Lad	So	Tees Real Grit	Jd
Lesterlin Gay	T	That's Rippin'	So
Levenside Luke	Jr	The President	So
Little Aristocrat	So	Trimmer	J
Milner	Jr	Venio	S
Monkshood	So	Vesuvian	S
Myrtus	So	Vibo	S
		Village Squire	Jd
		Viscount Dufferin	J
Netswell Rioter	Jd	Visto	S
Octavious	So	Warbreck Spero	Jd
Old Foiler	S	Waterman	So
Oppidan	Jr	Watteau Woodcock	T
Ordnance	Jd	Wattoford	Jr
Orkadian	So	Wellesley Duke	Jr
		Wrose Indelible	So